PATRIOTISM AND PACIFISM IN EARLY BRITISH PENTECOSTALISM
THE DIVERGENT VIEWS OF A.A. BODDY
AND A.S. BOOTH-CLIBBORN

PATRIOTISM AND PACIFISM
IN EARLY BRITISH PENTECOSTALISM

THE DIVERGENT VIEWS OF A.A. BODDY
AND A.S. BOOTH-CLIBBORN

GEOFF CRAVEN

Cherohala Press
Cleveland, Tennessee

Patriotism and Pacifism in Early British Pentecostalism
The Divergent Views of A.A. Boddy and A.S. Booth-Clibborn

Published by Cherohala Press
900 Walker ST NE
Cleveland, TN 37311
USA

ISBN-13: 978-1-935931-91-1

CONTENTS

ACKNOWLEDGEMENTS

In memory of my mother and father; from their example I learned to value the Scriptures; also of my father-in-law, pastor, church-planter, and pacifist; and mother-in-law who gave lifelong support to that ministry.

Thank you to my wife Ruth, for her patience during the time taken to research and write this book, and to my daughter Rachel, for proof-reading the manuscript.

To the administrators of the Donald Gee Research Centre, Mattersey Hall, thank you for making available to me the archived publications relevant to early Pentecostalism in Britain; also, to the staff at the Flower Pentecostal Heritage Centre, USA, for allowing me to access their relevant archives.

PREFACE

I was raised in a Christian family. My parents came to faith through the ministry of the Pentecostal evangelist Stephen Jeffries. My grandfather was killed at the Battle of the Somme, during the Great War. My father's uncle was a Methodist local-preacher, and pacifist at that time. Toy guns were generally banned in our home, but I remember taking part in a fancy-dress competition, at the age of eight, dressed as a Coldstream Guard, complete with a toy rifle having a silver-painted, fixed, wooden bayonet. My elder brother completed National Service in the British Army. In my later years, I came to find all of this quite confusing.

I first met my future father-in-law in 1962, and I listened to a careful exposition of his views on Christian pacifism, which were clearly focused upon Jesus' teaching, with examples drawn from Church History. In the war years (World War II, 1939-45), he had been a Conscientious Objector, securing unconditional exemption from military service on the basis of his Christian pacifist faith. In the years that followed he successfully defended a number of young men at their tribunals and court-martials, because of their decision to reject militarism. During the war, although at this time he and his wife had one child, they opened their home to accommodate five young evacuees from London, at their own expense – their living came from their modest fruit and flower business.

Out of these events, and my reflections upon them, the seeds of the research for this book were sown. The inspiration to write this book also flows from more than two-years of doctoral study; I felt compelled to write about this issue which was of deep significance within early Pentecostalism in Britain. The polarising and divisive views of patriotism and pacifism impacted upon the beliefs and practice, ethics and worldview, of early Pentecostals, both at that time, and since.

An examination is undertaken of patriotism and war, as portrayed in the life, and writing of Alexander Alfred Boddy (1854-1930). Boddy was the acknowledged founder/leader of early

Pentecostalism in Britain, with an influence in many countries beyond. He was an ordained Anglican minister.

The opposing argument in favour of Christian pacifism is outlined from an examination of the life and writing of Arthur Sydney Booth-Clibborn (1855-1939). Booth-Clibborn, the son-in-law of William Booth, founder of the Salvation Army, was a well-known figure within Quakerism in Ireland. He was a leader of the Salvation Army in Europe, and later he was European representative of the American, Alexander Dowie, and his healing movement. He became a prominent figure within early Pentecostalism in Britain.

The views of Boddy and Booth-Clibborn come under close scrutiny, and act as a catalyst for the discussion and argument of this book.

As the title of this book, *Patriotism and Pacifism within Early Pentecostalism in Britain,* suggests, there are two views to be explored and considered: Patriotism – where this leads to, or supports, militarism and war; and Christian pacifism, which implies all the opposites of patriotism and militarism. These opposing views are considered within the context of early Pentecostalism. Whilst other countries, particularly North America and Europe, have their own histories, the focus here is upon early Pentecostalism in Britain.

There is no wish or intention to belittle or discredit the significant ministries of either Boddy or Booth-Clibborn, but rather to critique their actions and written thoughts, in an attempt to understand their underlying beliefs and worldview, and their legacy for those that followed.

The book is ordered into Chapters as follows: the Introduction includes a brief examination of the nature of early Pentecostalism, and defines patriotism, and pacifism. The background and social / historical context of early Pentecostalism in Britain is also provided. Chapter 1 gives a short biographical profile of Boddy, which includes aspects of his life and ministry. Chapter 2 provides a biographical profile of Booth-Clibborn, which includes aspects of his life and ministry. Chapter 3 investigates the nature of Boddy's patriotism. Chapter 4 explores the nature of Booth-Clibborn's pacifism. Chapter 5 provides a critical assessment of Boddy's patriotism. Chapter 6 provides a critical assessment of Booth-Clibborn's pacifism. Chapter 7 examines the relationships between Quakersim and early Pentecostalism in Britain. Chapter 8 discusses the legacies of A.A. Boddy, and A.S. Booth-Clibborn. Chapter 9 considers the contemporary relevance and significance of patriotism and pacifism, whilst in Chapter 10, the last chapter, an attempt is made to draw some meaningful conclusions.

Because of the divisive nature of the issues of patriotism/militarism and pacifism within the Church and beyond, a priority here is to present insights into the issues involved, for the benefit of students, pastors, teachers, researchers, and others who may have an interest in the period of early Pentecostalism in Britain, or of Pentecostalism within the context of Church History. The issues raised in this book continued to be of significance to following generations of leaders, and believers, within Pentecostalism in Britain. It is envisaged that this book will prompt others to research this subject area further among the later generations of Pentecostal and Charismatic believers.

INTRODUCTION

Before exploring the cultural, social, and religious context of the latter part of the nineteenth century, and the years leading up to World War I (1914-1918), it is appropriate first to define the three important elements of this study, these are: Pentecostalism, patriotism, and pacifism.

Pentecostalism defined

There have been numerous attempts to define the nature of early Pentecostalism in Britain. William Kay and Anne Dyer, in their introduction to *Pentecostal and Charismatic Studies*, write:

> Since about 1900 the Pentecostal and charismatic movements have renewed, reformed and expanded great sections of Christianity. At the centre of these movements is an experience. It is the experience of the Holy Spirit similar to that enjoyed by members of the early Church on the day of Pentecost and described in the Bible in the book of Acts – at least that is what Pentecostals and charismatics, with good reason, claim. The experience issues in a variety of *charismata* or spiritual gifts, including speaking with other tongues or *glossalalia*.[1]

Attracting many new converts and believers drawn from a variety of mainstream Christian groups (Baptist, Independent, Methodist, Congregationalist, Anglican, and so on), the early Pentecostals claimed – in addition to: faith in Jesus Christ, repentance of sin,

---

[1] William K. Kay and Anne E. Dyer, *Pentecostal and Charismatic Studies* (London: SCM Press, 2004), p. xix.

forgiveness, salvation, and new life in Christ – the added dimension of an experience of the Holy Spirit, as described above. Early Pentecostal meetings frequently included elements of charismatic preaching, lively singing (which was often unaccompanied), harmonious praise, and inspirational worship. Opportunity for personal testimony and prayers for the sick featured in many church services. Having outlined something of the nature of early Pentecostalism, brief definitions of patriotism and pacifism follow.

Patriotism defined

A patriot is, 'one who strongly supports and serves his or her country'.[2] The term also implies a love for, and a loyalty to one's country. In a basic sense, one who follows the British football, rugby, or athletics teams, might be described as patriotic. Such a patriot expects the national team to win, by scoring more points or by winning more events, thereby defeating the teams of the countries in opposition. Patriotism, when referred to in this book implies the support of one's country when it engages in war and militarism. Patriotism was the widely held view in the latter part of the nineteenth-century, and in the years leading up to, and during, the Great War.

Pacifism defined

Pacifism, however, values all the opposites of patriotism, when patriotism leads to militarism. Pacifism works towards the abolition of all wars. A pacifist is one who advocates the abolition of all wars and refuses to take part in war.[3] A pacifist is interested, primarily, in creating, and maintaining peace. Andrew Goddard has provided a clear definition of pacifism:

> It must, however, not be forgotten that there is a long-standing pacifist strand in Christian history which advocates a renuncia-

---

[2] *New English Dictionary and Thesaurus* (New Lanark, Scotland: Geddes and Grosset Ltd, 1995), p. 438.
[3] *New English Dictionary and Thesaurus*, p. 430.

tion of all violence and participation in war on the part of Christians as a faithful witness to the way of Jesus Christ.[4]

Martin Ceadel cited Peter Brock, who claimed that pacifism is nearly two thousand years old.[5] Ceadel has summarized pacifism in the Early Church period:

> Members of the early Christian Church seem for the most part to have refused to fight in Roman armies, and Christian pacifists have always claimed that this attitude remains the most straightforward reading of Christian doctrine on war.[6]

Ceadel then added:

> … since AD 313, when the Emperor Constantine made Christianity the official religion of the Roman Empire, pacifism has been abandoned by the church in so far as the latter has agreed to support certain 'just' wars![7]

From this, it is clear that Christians were pacifists, from the earliest times of the Church.

The so-named 'Peace Churches', particularly the Mennonites, and Quakers, (the Society of Friends), have proved influential in the cause of Christian pacifism, particularly over the past four-hundred or so years; to such an extent that to be 'a Quaker', would in most cases be taken to mean a pacifist, so strong was the association. The social/political influences of pacifism are identified by Peter Brock and Nigel Young; they observed, 'socialist anti-militarism, which emerged, along with the organised labour movement in the half century before 1914',[8] in Britain. It is appropriate now to outline the wider context of this period of British history.

---

[4] Andrew Goddard, *When is War Justified?* (Cambridge: Grove Books, 2003), p. 3.

[5] Martin Ceadel, *Pacifism in Britain 1914-1945: The Defining of a Faith* (Oxford: Clarendon Press, 1980), p. 18, citing Peter Brock, *Pacifism in Europe*, p. 3.

[6] Ceadel, *Pacifism in Britain*, p. 19.

[7] Ceadel, *Pacifism in Britain*, p. 19.

[8] Peter Brock & Nigel Young, *Pacifism in the Twentieth Century* (New York: Syracuse University Press, 1999), p. 4.

Education

By the mid-nineteenth century, the majority of people in Britain
were illiterate. Birth and marriage certificates were authenticated
with a mark, rather than with a signature. With full credit to successive governments and their initiatives, enormous progress was made
to correct this situation of mass illiteracy: Sunday Schools[9] grew at
a rapid rate; by the end of the nineteenth century, they had contributed significantly to the provision of basic and religious education
of 6 million children, 80 per cent of children between the ages of
five and fourteen. The Education Act of 1870 empowered local
school boards to build and manage schools.[10] Schools and Sunday
Schools had a combined impact in this period to the extent that by
1893, 95 per cent (approx) of newly-married couples were able to
sign their names in the marriage register.[11] Whilst the state schools
developed and were successful in their provision of the much
needed education of young people, public schools also prospered
in this period. By the 1860's, nine large schools were established,[12]
and by the end of the century a hundred or so public schools were
established. Overall, their aims were to train boys, socially and in-
tellectually, for leadership in government, in the church, and for service in the armed forces at home and overseas. This point is made
in James Hilton's *Goodbye Mr Chipps*,[13] the fictional story-line which
is focussed upon the life and work of a Latin tutor, Mr Chipping,
in the period of the 1880's–1930's, at Brookfield School, which indicated that in the years leading up to WWI, public schools became
training and recruiting grounds for the armed forces. Brookfield
School was no exception: a man of senior military rank was employed for a period as headmaster; his sole purpose was to intro-
duce patriotic militarism to the school.

---

[9] Founded in 1769 by Hannah Ball, developed by Robert Raikes, 'Awakening'
by A. Skevington Wood, in Dowley, T. *et al.* (eds.), *The History of Christianity* (Oxford: Lion, 1990), p. 452.

[10] David Hey, *How Our Ancestors Lived: A History of Life a Hundred Years Ago*
(Kew: The National Archives, 2003), p. 113.

[11] Hey, *How Our Ancestors Lived*, p. 114.

[12] At: Eton, Harrow, Winchester, Shrewsbury, Westminster, St. Paul's, Mer-
chant Taylor's, Charterhouse, and Rugby. In Hey, *How Our Ancestors Lived*, p. 114.

[13] James Hilton, *Goodbye Mr Chipps* (London: Hodder & Stoughton, 1934).

At the turn of the century, the Boer War, and within a few years, World War I, could hardly have been expected or anticipated. For many young men, their lives would be severely tested by these events.

The Nonconformists

The church historian Donald Durnbaugh, has noted that the term 'free church' was first used in England as a designation for those churches of dissent which were separate from the state.[14]

Further, 'the Nonconformist grouping normally included Presbyterians, Congregationalists, Methodists, Quakers and Baptists',[15] with Quakers and Baptists on the left wing of dissent.[16] For example, the Quakers' testimony against slavery during the nineteenth-century proved to be a major factor in its abolition.[17]

From the national census of religious worship undertaken in 1851, it is seen that the Nonconformist groups were enjoying significant growth. More than half the population did not attend any form of religious worship, and of those who did attend, more than half preferred a chapel service to the one held by the Church of England.[18] Nonconformist chapels had been built at an increasing rate during the first half of the nineteenth-century: the Wesleyans had 825 chapels in 1801, but there were 11,007 fifty years later. Baptist chapels had risen in number, from 652 to 2,789 in the same period; the Congregationalists from 914 to 3,244.[19] These figures serve to illustrate the enormous efforts made, and the substantial church-growth achieved in this period. The chapels, in particular, were the local centres of social and communal life. The Boy's Brigade, the Church Lad's Brigade, men's fellowships, women's guilds, choral societies, and sports clubs, were all church or chapel based.[20]

---

[14] Donald Durnbaugh, *The Believers' Church* (Scottdale, PA: Herald Press, 1968, 1985), p. 5.

[15] Durnbaugh, *The Believers' Church*, p. 16.

[16] Durnbaugh, *The Believers' Church*, p. 97.

[17] Durnbaugh, *The Believers' Church*, p. 241.

[18] Hey, *How Our Ancestors Lived*, p. 120.

[19] Hey, *How Our Ancestors Lived*, p. 121.

[20] Hey, *How Our Ancestors Lived*, p. 123.

From the 1901 census figures[21], the Nonconformist groups out-numbered the Established Church by around 40 per cent at this time in Britain. The established church employed 25,235 clergymen, and the Nonconformist groups registered 11,572. In all cases, a growth in numbers was registered: in the Nonconformist groups around 15 per cent, in the Established Church around 4 per cent. In England and Wales, the struggle between church and chapel was one of the great political issues of the period.

It might be anticipated that any new radical evangelical group emerging at around this time would have been from among the left-wing Nonconformists. That was not to be the case with early Pentecostalism, although many believers from Nonconformist groups would join; its beginnings were established in the Church of England, the State-Church.

The Empire

Hey reported that by the end of the century,

> the British Empire covered more than one-fifth of the world's land mass, with a population of 400 million; little more than one-tenth of this population lived in Britain. Much of the Empire had been acquired in the last quarter of the nineteenth- century.[22]

It is seen that Britain had expanded rapidly across the world. Whilst at home, the country enjoyed the relative stability of a long-reigning monarch,[23] there was much poverty across Britain, but the opposite was also true, that some enjoyed great wealth.

By 1861, the population of the Empire was estimated at 175 million; by the end of the twentieth-century, it had reached more than 400 million.[24] The British Empire had expanded into Africa,

---

[21] From these statistics, the Church of England claimed to have 2,796,000 members; the Church in Wales 141,008; the Scottish Episcopal Church 116,296; and the Church of Ireland 296,000. The Presbyterian organisation, the Church of Scotland recorded 661,629 members; other Presbyterians and Congregationalists numbered 1,238,499 members; the Baptists 1,945,128; the Methodists 728,289 in England; 33,926 in Wales; 8,191 in Scotland, and 27,745 in Ireland.

[22] Hey, *How Our Ancestors Lived*, p. 139.

[23] Queen Victoria (1819-1901) reigned as Queen (1837-1901).

[24] Hey, *How Our Ancestors Lived*, p. 144.

India, Canada, Australia, and New Zealand. During the last 40 years of the nineteenth-century, the Empire had increased in size by 50 per cent. In order to support this expansion, each political party at home had an imperialist wing, whose purpose was to keep all the associated issues in view.

Hey records, 'the end of the nineteenth-century saw the Empire overstretched and under-defended'.[25] The South African Boer War (1899-1902), cost Britain more than £200 million, with more than 100,000 casualties from both sides. This war signalled that the limits of Britain's imperial expansion had been reached.[26]

This then was the background and context into which Alexander Alfred Boddy and Arthur Sydney Clibborn were born. They would, from their youth, both become deeply involved in the religious lives of their communities. Boddy within the Anglican Church, Clibborn within non-conformist groups.

---

[25] Hey, *How Our Ancestors Lived*, p. 144.
[26] Hey, *How Our Ancestors Lived*, p. 144.

1

A.A. BODDY (1854-1930): BIOGRAPHICAL NOTES

Alexander Alfred Boddy was born on 15th November 1854, into an Anglican minister's family. His father, James Alfred Boddy (1810–1881), was appointed Rector at Cheetham, Manchester in 1844, staying there through to 1871,[1] at which time he moved to the North East of England.

Boddy, 'joined Manchester Grammar School, in January 1868',[2] at the age of fourteen. 'He was confirmed by the Bishop of Manchester, on the 10th October 1870',[3] at age sixteen. Boddy left Manchester Grammar School to join Worsley & Parker, Solicitors. At age 21, he became assistant solicitor in 1876. Following his training and placement, Boddy qualified as a lawyer/solicitor.[4] Boddy, later recalled that he spent seven years in this work.[5]

Boddy's father moved from Manchester to Elwick Hall, Castle Eden, County Durham, to become Rector, in October 1871.[6] Appointed as Curate at Elwick Hall, Alexander was able to help his sick father. His father died in March 1881.[7] Following his father's

---

[1] *Crockfords Clerical Directory* (London: Horace Cox, 1880).
[2] Gavin Wakefield, *Alexander Boddy Pentecostal Anglican Pioneer* (London: Paternoster, 2007), p. 15.
[3] Wakefield, *Boddy*, p. 15.
[4] Wakefield, *Boddy*, pp. 15-16.
[5] *Confidence* 13.2 (Jan-Mar 1923), p. 6.
[6] *Crockfords Clerical Directory*, 1880.
[7] Wakefield, *Boddy*, p. 25.

death, Boddy served as Curate at St. Helens, Low Fell; then to be Curate at St. Peter's in Bishop Auckland, 1884.[8]

After visiting the Keswick Convention in 1876, Boddy felt constrained to pursue the ordained ministry within the Church of England. During this process, he was encouraged by Bishop J.B. Lightfoot. In 1878, Boddy studied at Durham University for the Licentiate in Theology; a two-year course with the objective of ordination. In 1880, just prior to the completion of his course of study, Bishop Lightfoot made him a deacon.[9]

Boddy was appointed vicar of All Saints Anglican Church, Monkwearmouth, Sunderland, in 1886; he stayed through to 1922, at which time he moved to the Church of St Lawrence, Pittington Hallgarth, Durham, staying there until his death on 10th September 1930.[10]

Boddy was an experienced traveller and travel writer, and in 1885 was appointed a member of the Royal Geographical Society; two years later, he was appointed Fellow of the same society. Not least due to his adventurous spirit, he took every opportunity to travel, making detailed records of his experiences. In the years of the late nineteenth and early twentieth century, Boddy was inspired to follow church revivals as they emerged in: South Wales, Los Angeles, Norway, and other places. Boddy was well-equipped to undertake the combined task of travel and writing/reporting, and he travelled extensively, he met many people, and attended numerous events.

Boddy sought God for such a revival in his own church, similar to the ones that he had witnessed. He launched the Sunderland Annual Convention in 1908, with the stated aim of the conference: 'To honour Jesus and to keep closer and closer to His Word'.[11]

At around this time, Boddy launched *Confidence,* a newspaper serving early Pentecostalism. He was controlling editor and publisher for a lengthy period, (1908-1926). Of this, Wakefield observed:

---

[8] Wakefield, *Boddy*, p. 25.
[9] Wakefield, *Boddy*, p. 24.
[10] Gavin Wakefield, *The First Pentecostal Anglican* (Cambridge: Grove Books, 2001), p. 24.
[11] *Confidence* 1.2 (May 1908), p. 5.

In Britain, his leadership was exercised through his writing ministry and through the numerous conventions in which he became involved, most importantly, the annual Whitsuntide Conferences and Conventions'.[12]

Boddy hosted and convened the early conventions at his church, All Saints, Sunderland, from 1908. In her short biographical memoir of her father, Jane Vazeille Boddy depicted the early days of the Sunderland Convention, as both international and ecumenical.[13] This was a fitting tribute to Boddy's efforts.

A perusal of Boddy's writing in the *Confidence* newspaper provides many clues as to what his key themes, beliefs, and theology consisted of: he believed in the supremacy of Jesus Christ and the effectiveness of his death on Calvary. He frequently asserted that the work of God's Spirit in a believer's life produced love. In the mature years of his ministry, Boddy majored on the theme of love. For example, his assertion that 'the first fruit of the Spirit is love' is mentioned in numerous places throughout the issues of *Confidence*.[14]

Wakefield has observed:

Boddy ultimately had an instinct; still felt by many Anglicans, that unity in love was more important than absolute precision in doctrine.[15]

Boddy proved to be a capable leader and facilitator within early Pentecostalism in Britain. He insisted on respect for the leader at the annual conferences, and that the operation of spiritual gifts among believers be orderly, so as not to bring a bad reputation among those who did not attend, or controversy among those who did. For many years, Boddy served on the Pentecostal Missionary Union Council, but this is part of the movement's history of overseas missions and lies outside of the scope of this book.

Boddy was a faithful pastor, long-serving, and loved by his flock, also by those of other denominations. Apart from his daily duties serving in a busy Anglican parish, Boddy found the time to attend,

---

[12] Wakefield, *Boddy*, p. 103.

[13] Jane Vazeille Boddy, 'Alexander Alfred Boddy', Biographical Notes, p. 8, courtesy of Flower Pentecostal Heritage, USA.

[14] *Confidence* 7.2 (Feb. 1914), p. 24.

[15] Wakefield, *Boddy*, p. 214.

and to organise conferences, edit and publish *Confidence,* speak at other churches when requested, and undertake a range of ecumenical activities. Boddy also found the time to engage with the issue of temperance. Wakefield has observed that Boddy was, 'a lifelong teetotaller, and active in the Church of England Temperance Society'.[16]

Of her father's parish work, Boddy's daughter Jane Vazeille Boddy reflected:

> There was a lot of drunkenness in our neighbourhood, especially at the week-ends, and on Saturday nights my father used to go round the public houses and take the drunken men home.[17]

Jane Vazeille Boddy further recorded that her Father held open-air services outside one of the public houses, following the Sunday evening church service.[18]
And again:

> He was wonderful with the sick and dying and was often called out at night to minister to them.[19]

In all of his pastoral endeavours, Boddy clearly identified with his many parishioners, offering both practical and spiritual help, and support.

Chapters 3 and 5 are devoted to Boddy's patriotism, aspects of the Great War, his views of it, and his participation in it as a Chaplain to the troops.

---

[16] Wakefield, *Boddy*, p. 29.
[17] Boddy, Notes, p. 3.
[18] Boddy, Notes, p. 3.
[19] Boddy, Notes, p. 4.

2

A.S. BOOTH-CLIBBORN (1855-1939): BIOGRAPHICAL NOTES

Arthur Sydney Clibborn, was born into an Irish, Quaker family in Moate, County Westmeath, but spent his formative years in Bessbrook, County Armagh. He was a capable scholar, writer, and hymn-writer. Clibborn was educated in France and Switzerland from the age of 13 years, and later received the award of an honours degree from Lausanne University.[1] He later referred to his education, and the time when his father, a Quaker, took him to school in Switzerland, in 1868.[2] He could speak four languages.[3]

Following training, he was employed as a manager in the family business in Bessbrook. Of this period, Clibborn wrote:

> Myself the son of a manufacturer, having learnt to weave and spin with my own hands, having had at one time eleven hundred workmen under my direction, each of whose machines I had been myself trained to run, and having once caught a finger in the cog wheels, I may be able to speak with some knowledge, both of working men and of working machinery.[4]

---

[1] James Robinson, 'Arthur Booth-Clibborn: Pentecostal Patriarch', *Journal of the European Pentecostal Theological Association* 21 (2001), pp. 68-70.
[2] A.S. Booth-Clibborn, *Blood Against Blood* (New York: Charles Cook, 1914), p. 65.
[3] Booth-Clibborn, *Blood Against Blood*, p. 65.
[4] Booth-Clibborn, *Blood Against Blood*, pp. 90-91.

This serves to illustrate Clibborn's extensive experience of work-ing in the family's textile business. His father, James Clibborn, was co-founder of the linen mills at Bessbrook,[5] and he had entered business with Quaker relatives, founders and owners of the Model Temperance Town of Bessbrook in Northern Ireland; [6] a town of about two-thousand inhabitants; called a model town, having nei-ther public house, police station, or pawn shop. Clibborn recalls seeing the light of salvation during revival meetings at Moyallon, some fourteen miles from his home.[7] His wife Catherine (Kate)[8], later recorded of this period:

> He was soundly converted during the Moody Revival in 1875 ... and was baptised in the Spirit two years later ... the result that a remarkable revival took place under his ministry[9] ... From the converts, preachers went out all over the world. This work soon attracted attention, and he was recorded a minister of the Soci-ety of Friends at an unusually young age.[10]

This indicated that Clibborn was well suited to evangelistic and pastoral work. The family biographer, Carolyn Scott, observed, that 'by the time he was twenty-six, he not only had eleven hundred workers under his control, but had been appointed the youngest Quaker minister for over a hundred years.'[11]

When Clibborn took about thirty of his young men, all new con-verts to Christianity, to Salvation Army Holiness meetings at Moy-allon; it was there, following a revelation, that Clibborn's heart cried out, 'here is primitive Methodism, primitive Quakerism, primitive Christianity!'[12]

Clibborn was persuaded by the General [William Booth], who conferred on him the rank of Colonel. Clibborn then served as a

---

[5] Carolyn Scott, *The Heavenly Witch: the Story of the Maréchale* (London: Hamish Hamilton, 1981), p. 47.

[6] Catherine Booth, *A Poet of Praise: A Tribute to Arthur Sydney Booth-Clibborn* (London: Marshall, Morgan & Scott, c.1939), p.13.

[7] Scott, *The Heavenly Witch*, p. 50.

[8] Hereafter referred to as Kate, so as to avoid confusion with her mother, also Catherine.

[9] Booth, *A Poet of Praise*, p. 1.

[10] Booth, *A Poet of Praise*, pp. 13-14.

[11] Scott, *The Heavenly Witch*, p. 47.

[12] Scott, *The Heavenly Witch*, p. 53.

missionary and evangelist to mainland Europe in the Salvation Army. He worked as a Regional Director, alongside William Booth's daughter, Kate, where in France he assisted her with the production of the French *War Cry*.[13] Kate Booth and Arthur Sydney Clibborn were married, Tuesday, 8th February 1887, at the Congress Hall, Clacton. A few days prior to the wedding, Arthur changed his name by deed poll, to Arthur Sydney Booth-Clibborn.[14] Of her husband's call to work for the Salvation Army, Kate wrote:

> General and Mrs William Booth pressed him to enter the Salvation Army. Sacrificing his career, and bidding farewell to his converts in Ireland, he accepted the challenge, and took up work on the Continent, for which he was eminently suited, as he spoke four languages fluently.[15]

When Booth-Clibborn was called to serve in the Salvation Army, in 1881, his Quaker upbringing and faith led him to assert, 'I could never forego any of the essential truths of Quakerism, and I entered the work on that understanding'.[16] The Booth-Clibborn's laboured successfully, but with significant opposition, in France and Switzerland. In spite of the opposition, they were able to establish numerous corps (congregations of Salvation Army believers and followers) across both countries. These groups in later years received annual visits from Kate.[17]

Scott, recorded one incident that enhanced the popularity of Kate and Arthur: Arthur received a silver medal award, from the President of France, to honour his courage in going to the rescue of a French life; he saved a man from drowning in the sea; an example of his bravery against enormous odds.[18]

The Booth-Clibborn's held a great love and respect for each other. This is apparent when Kate, many years later, reflected that her husband had been, 'a valiant and intensely loyal soldier of the Cross'. [19]

---

[13] Scott, *The Heavenly Witch*, p. 47.
[14] Scott, *The Heavenly Witch*, p. 155.
[15] Booth, *A Poet of Praise*, pp. 13-14.
[16] Scott, *The Heavenly Witch*, p. 54.
[17] Scott, *The Heavenly Witch*, p. 164.
[18] Scott, *The Heavenly Witch*, pp. 166-67.
[19] Booth, *A Poet of Praise*, p. 13.

Scott picks up on the theme of Booth-Clibborn's Quaker ancestry, and pacifism, stating: 'because like all Quakers, he was an ardent pacifist'.[20] Booth's pacifist views were a non-negotiable element of his Quaker faith and upbringing. He understood his family's long Quaker tradition; he possessed an encyclopaedic knowledge of the Bible; he had a clear grasp of Christian history, and all of these he applied to his own understanding of what pacifism meant to him in terms of both faith and practice.

During 1891, Arthur wrote to the General 'requesting freedom to preach the full, plain Gospel of the Sermon on the Mount'. This included pacifism, healing, and the Second Coming of Jesus Christ.[21] Arthur never received an answer to his request from the General. Some fifteen years later, 'at the beginning of 1896 orders came through from the International Headquarters in London for Kate and Arthur to leave France and Switzerland, to take command in Holland or Germany'.[22] This was disturbing news, as they had worked successfully in France. It soon became apparent that the order had been sent from Bramwell Booth – General Booth being away on tour at the time.[23] When the Booth-Clibborns visited the General in order to discuss this issue, along with Arthur's wish to preach the full gospel (he had raised this issue some fifteen years before), they were refused.[24] The Booth-Clibborn's would later leave the Salvation Army because they could not reach agreement with William Booth on the issues of relocation to Holland or Germany, and of preaching the full gospel. General Booth had decided that he wanted the Salvation Army to maintain a non-pacifist position. At this time, pacifism was often seen as being anti-government. It was also possible that Booth did not wish to upset the government, which had allowed the Salvation Army permission to visit public-houses on a frequent basis, for the purpose of distributing the *War Cry* magazine, thereby raising funds, so necessary for their work to continue.

Following his time with the Salvation Army, Booth-Clibborn worked with the healing evangelist, John Alexander Dowie (1847-

---

[20] Scott, *The Heavenly Witch*, p. 48.
[21] Scott, *The Heavenly Witch*, p. 179.
[22] Scott, *The Heavenly Witch*, p. 177.
[23] Scott, *The Heavenly Witch*, p. 178.
[24] Scott, *The Heavenly Witch*, p. 187.

1907), for a two-year period. Dowie inspired Booth-Clibborn: he was a powerful leader and speaker; he espoused pacifism, and divine healing also. He was instrumental in building a large community at Zion City, IL USA. Booth-Clibborn had lived and worked in such a community in Bessbrook, and this held a certain appeal. However, things did not work out with Dowie and Booth-Clibborn's wife, Kate, and so it was decided that Booth-Clibborn would work for Dowie as European representative.

The Booth-Clibborn's later settled in England where they enjoyed fellowship with the leaders and believers within early Pentecostalism. By 1909, aged 54, he had become a well-known and respected figure within the movement in Britain. At a convention meeting at Sion College in London, in May of that year, he shared the platform with Alexander Boddy, Cecil Polhill, and Thomas Ball Barratt.[25] Polhill was a leading figure in the Pentecostal Missionary Union, whilst Barratt was church-planting in Sweden, and other places in Northern Europe. Booth-Clibborn came late to Pentecostalism. He wished to avoid further involvement with organisations, and the early stirrings of Pentecostalism appealed to him.

Following the Boer War (1899-1902), Booth-Clibborn felt prompted to write his overtly pacifist, and controversial book, *Blood against Blood*, first published in 1907. As WWI approached, he revised the book in 1914, for a wider audience; the work was published on both sides of the Atlantic and proved to be greatly influential to young men deliberating about their faith and the issue of war. It was accepted within the Assemblies of God, a group within Pentecostalism in America, as a serious pacifist work.

Booth-Clibborn's pacifist views are discussed in Chapters 4 and 6.

---

[25] Robinson, 'Arthur Booth-Clibborn', p. 69, citing A.F. Missen, *The Sound of a Going* (Nottingham: AOG, 1974), p. 4.

3

BODDY'S PATRIOTISM

This Chapter outlines Boddy's patriotic views from his written reports and activities depicted in the pages of *Confidence* – he was its publisher and editor-in-chief. Whilst Gavin Wakefield[1] has suggested that Boddy's patriotism was commensurate with Germany's initiation of the Great War by its invasion of Belgium, Boddy's rhetoric, writing, and experiences, suggest that his views on patriotism and militarism were formed at a much earlier time in his life.

Boddy had an adventurous spirit, and it appears that his patriotic views were an integral part of that. In numerous pages of *Confidence,* Boddy revealed that he had no problem with the use of militarism as a means of resolving national or international disputes. Boddy tried to instil his own adventurous spirit in his children.[2] This was later evidenced when his son became an aviator – he was shot down in an air raid over France during WWI.

Wakefield records that Boddy visited a warship in the waters off Sunderland.[3] Boddy's daughter, Jane Vazeille Boddy, recalling this incident, wrote:

Once when a war-ship was anchored out beyond the pier, and visitors were invited, he rowed us out to it, though there was a very *rough* sea and no one else took the risk. We were all sea-sick, but my father was perfectly happy and quite unconcerned at the

---

[1] Gavin Wakefield, *Alexander Boddy, Pentecostal Anglican Pioneer* (London: Paternoster Press, 2007), pp. 183-84.

[2] Wakefield, *Boddy*, p. 57.

[3] Wakefield, *Boddy*, p. 58.

storm! So we were shown all over the ship and given a good tea before we ventured back![4]

On one occasion, Boddy noted the positioning of ships' flags.[5] This suggests that he had both an interest in, and a keen eye for, matters of maritime and national significance. Again, on this, Jane Vazeille Boddy provides some detail; she reflected that her father 'loved ships and knew all about them'. Also, 'that he had helped to start the Seamen's Mission in Sunderland and always supported it whole-heartedly.[6]

When Boddy was on a trip to North Africa, and whilst in Valetta, Malta, during 1883, at the age of 29, he 'took realistic precautions for the journey ahead, by buying a six-barrelled revolver and a thick serviceable stick'.[7] This was for the purpose of his personal defence and protection.

Boddy's patriotic feelings were illustrated by his numerous published entries in *Confidence* where articles appeared under a variety of headings, for example, 'With our troops in France', and 'The War'. Boddy placed importance upon soldiers in general and included those that he referred to as Christian soldiers and Pentecostal soldiers,[8] and he published a number of their letters in *Confidence*. In Boddy's North Star newspaper interview, he indicated that when in France as an honorary Chaplain during WWI, he was 'encouraging our soldiers in the camps'.[9] Boddy described British troops as 'cheery, nice fellows',[10] and 'good comrades, hard-worked workers, doing their bit splendidly'. Referring to a soldier he met, he reported, 'he was glad as he went on with his guns, to take a Red Gospel with him'.[11]

Reporting from France, Boddy wrote:

They will soon be in the firing line. They are on the last lap of their journey. Days of training are over, and the longed-for call

---

[4] Boddy, Notes, p. 4.
[5] *Confidence* 2.6 (June 1909), p. 140.
[6] Boddy, Notes, p. 4.
[7] Wakefield, *Boddy*, p. 36, citing A.A. Boddy, *Kairwan*, p. 25.
[8] *Confidence* 7.9 (Sept. 1914), pp. 163-65.
[9] *Confidence* 8.6 (June. 1915), p. 107.
[10] *Confidence* 9.1 (Jan 1916), p. 3.
[11] *Confidence* 9.1 (Jan. 1916), p. 4.

to the front has come. They go up full of joy. There is wonderful comradeship in the trenches.[12]

Boddy included a letter in *Confidence* from a soldier in France, writing about his aspirations:

I have made a great sacrifice in giving up my freedom to go on long service for my king and country, but I mean to come back a good and true soldier, not only to serve my earthly king, but also my heavenly king.[13]

Boddy encouraged his *Confidence* readers with a comment: 'Let soldier and civilian turn to God, he will help'.[14]

Boddy reported on a Military Service that he conducted at All Saints Church, Sunderland, with soldiers and arms.[15] Boddy lamented his Christian friends in Germany, and stated:

We in turn are quite sure that our dear friends – we mean the more deeply spiritual Christians in Germany – cannot have had the truth made clear to them … we will pray for victory![16]

Boddy published a lengthy letter from G.R. Polman of Amsterdam. The letter reported on the work among soldiers in Germany, Belgium, and England. Visits had been made by, 'Arthur Booth-Clibborn, George Jeffries, Dr Phair, and others'. This group of pacifists explained to their audience that they had nothing to do with the war effort but had come to bring the Gospel of Christ.[17] Immediately following Polman's letter, Boddy published a pro-war article by Pastor W. Graham Scroggie, in which he asserted:

To say 'War is of the devil, and in principle and practice is entirely anti-Christian', is to take refuge from one's obligations behind a generalisation which is half a truth and half a lie. To ask,

---

[12] *Confidence* 8.11 (Nov. 1915), p. 212.
[13] *Confidence* 7.9 (Sept. 1914), p. 165.
[14] *Confidence* 7.10 (Oct. 1914), p. 192.
[15] *Confidence* 8.1 (Jan. 1915), p. 4.
[16] *Confidence* 7.11 (Nov.1914), p. 14.
[17] *Confidence* 7.11 (Nov. 1914), p. 205.

'Should a Christian go to war?' is to raise a question of considerable importance, of thought and fact.[18]

Scroggie continued that 'we greatly respect the attitude of the "Friends" [the Quakers] towards that dread thing we call war', but he strongly disagreed with their position. He went on to justify war, from the Old Testament. He gave an example of a bully terrorising first a little child, and then a whole village; (Germany is the bully; the child is Belgium; the villagers are countries of Europe).[19] It is obvious from the outset that he was well aware of the overt pacifism of the Quakers, probably the views of Booth-Clibborn also. In the full transcript of his article, Scroggie, was arguably, dismissive of aspects of the Ten Commandments, and of the teaching of Jesus, as recorded in the Gospels.

Boddy made no secret of his rejection of Christian pacifist faith,[20] and this never seemed far from the surface in his writing. When pacifist Arthur Booth-Clibborn (the writer of more than 300 hymns), submitted alternative lyrics for the chorus of the tune Tipperary, Boddy published these in *Confidence*, but then added an alternative version of his own, with the assertion that his version was for use by soldiers and Christian men when they were marching.[21] In the later pages of the same issue of *Confidence*, Boddy indicated that 'my honoured brother in the Lord, A.S. Booth-Clibborn, would like me to recommend his book against War, entitled *Blood Against Blood*'. Boddy then challenged the book's validity by adding a counter-argument, 'most of us hate War, but many of us could not stand by calmly and see a murderer killing children without doing all that we could to prevent, to punish, and to incapacitate'. This statement by Boddy, expressed his major, if not only, argument for patriotism/militarism. Following this statement, he included a reference to a book title, *Britain Justified – the War from a Christian Standpoint*, a pro-war book by Frank Ballard. Boddy then underlined his patriotic position by assuring his readers that this book had been recommended

---

[18] *Confidence* 7.11 (Nov. 1914), pp. 205-207, citing Scroggie's article in the *Bethesda Record*.

[19] *Confidence* 7.11 (Nov 1914), pp. 205-207.

[20] A term used by Martin Ceadel, in *Pacifism in Britain 1914-1945: The Defining of a Faith* (Oxford: Clarendon Press, 1980).

[21] *Confidence* 8.1 (Jan. 1915), p. 5

and contained 'some striking statements'.[22] Boddy, in this way, used his editorial position, to endorse patriotic and pro-war views.

In the period of the Sunderland Conventions, Boddy and Booth-Clibborn might have been described as co-workers within early Pentecostalism. This is pictured by Boddy's daughter, Jane Vazeille Boddy, when she reflected:

> My father had a great admiration of General [William] Booth and on two occasions we had Mr. Booth-Clibborn, his son-in-law, at a convention. The second time he brought two of his sons and a daughter and they were all much impressed (they had left the Salvation Army).[23]

It is possible that Boddy was aware of the reasons for Booth-Clibborn's departure from the Salvation Army, and of the General's position against pacifism within his organisation.

There appeared to be a general cooling of Boddy's attitude towards pacifists as time progressed; his relationship with Booth-Clibborn also.

Boddy requested that his American readers of *Confidence* send to him 'interesting articles' about the War.[24] Presumably, he wished to see such articles, with a view to their publication. Boddy included an article by the Bishop of Durham, in which the Bishop asserted:

> We should pray ... for the fullest success, the most decisive victory, on the Allied side. As firmly as ever I hold that the War is a Holy War. I thank God that Britain never drew sword with hands more nobly white and clean.[25]

Boddy asked the readers of *Confidence* to pray: 'We believe God is on OUR side. But each one should ask "Am I on God's side?" What is He saying to me in these awful days?'[26] Could Boddy be questioning his own patriotism here, or is he questioning the pacifist position? This is not clear.

Boddy made the distinction between British heroes and German soldiers and officers. This illustrates the depth of Boddy's patriot-

---

[22] *Confidence* 8.1 (Jan. 1915), p. 6.
[23] Boddy, Notes, p. 8.
[24] *Confidence* 8.1 (Jan. 1915), p. 6.
[25] *Confidence* 8.1 (Jan. 1915), pp. 5-6.
[26] *Confidence* 8.5 (May. 1915), p. 91.

ism/militarism and lies at the core of what he believed. He wrote, 'Our British heroes lie buried, and also a number of German soldiers and officers'.[27]

Boddy suggested that through prayer, 'militarism may come to an end through this war'.[28] He went on to publish a letter from Pastor Voget at Bunde in which the pastor wrote, 'there is no war in Christ Jesus and in his true body ... united by the blood of Jesus, saved from the war-spirit'.[29] Voget's letter clearly expressed pacifist views.

On his time spent as a chaplain with the British troops in France, Boddy recollected: 'A very interesting time I had with the soldiers off duty in our Tent'.[30] He added, 'Up the hill came the guns and among the British gunners I made friends and had talks in the great YMCA tent'.[31] Boddy summarised his experiences as a chaplain in France:

> As I close the story of two months of privilege and opportunity, I would like to 'salute' my brave-fellow-countrymen who amid danger, dirt and discouragement, are bravely and often brightly standing firm. My beloved brothers – if my words can reach any of you – we thank you and are praying that our God will bring you home again safe and pure, unhurt in body and in soul. Be true to the Lord, who can give the Victory, to individuals and to nations if only there is 'Confidence' in Him.[32]

Boddy further wrote:

> Many special memorial services have been held by the Editor of *Confidence* for fallen British soldiers, etc., who have gone out from Sunderland. One of the latest was for a torpedoed engineer parishioner. Along this coast in war time there are constant dangers from submarines and mines. Our sailors are brave men, every moment running tremendous risks.[33]

---

27 *Confidence* 8.8 (Aug. 1915), p. 145.
28 *Confidence* 7.10 (Oct. 1914), p. 191.
29 *Confidence* 7.10 (Oct. 1914), p. 191.
30 *Confidence* 9.1 (Jan. 1916), p. 4.
31 *Confidence* 9.1 (Jan. 1916), p. 4.
32 *Confidence* 9.1 (Jan. 1916), p. 5.
33 *Confidence* 11.4 (Oct-Dec. 1918), p. 70.

Boddy reported on events during a service at All Saints Church, Sunderland: When 'preaching that morning there came the roar of aeroplanes nearby rushing up into the sky'. He stated that he was reminded of the Avenging Angels, and Angels of Deliverance, and continued, 'we thank God for the bravery of our airmen. They do their duty nobly to protect us from such scenes as we witnessed here, when women and children were killed and torn to pieces by the German bombs.' He reported further on, young Captain Ball (who laid down his life after putting about fifty hostile planes out of action) and his letter to his mother, which stated:

> I am indeed looked after by God; but oh, I get tired of always living to kill. I shall be so pleased when I have finished.[34]

Boddy continued his pro-war deliberations with a defence of Sir Edward Grey, Secretary of State for Foreign Affairs in Britain.[35] Grey had been denounced by the German Press. Boddy saw this as an affront, and an attempt at character assassination.

Boddy included a letter, under the title, 'What the USA thinks'. Part of this letter reads:

> Believing that this war is God's hand upon these nations in judgement for their national sins and that very prominent among the national sins of the Allies is that of intemperance, I am profoundly impressed that God will not give us the victory until this sin is put away from us.[36]

Mary Boddy's article in Confidence, under her husband's heading, 'The War', put forward the view that the War is a 'Spiritual War, a War of the Devil against Christ'[37] In his article, 'The War', Boddy asserted that:

> England has held back with all its might from this War, but now forced into it, the whole nation seems uplifted, and the Colonies have eagerly rallied to the support of an Empire which brings freedom – not militarism.[38]

---

[34] *Confidence* 11.4 (Oct-Dec. 1918), p. 70.
[35] *Confidence* 8.4 (April 1915), p. 28.
[36] *Confidence* 11.2 (April-June 1918), p. 32.
[37] *Confidence* 7.9 (Sept. 1914), p. 170.
[38] *Confidence* 8.1 (Jan. 1915), p. 4.

Boddy asserted that in this War, 'we believe that God is on our side'.[39] In the same issue of *Confidence*, Boddy included a letter from G.R. Polman of Amsterdam, in which he stated, 'It is not from a national standpoint that we are looking upon this war, but from God's standpoint'.[40]

In June 1915, Boddy announced to his *Confidence* readership, 'I have arranged to spread my vacation in June and July in France – visiting the wounded and encouraging our soldiers in the camps'.[41] In the later pages of the same issue, Boddy reported on the London Convention:

> Very earnest prayer concerning the War went up during the last day. The writer at the afternoon meeting appealed to the Pentecostal people to pray down on our soldiers and sailors salvation in this time of cruel conflict, and asked for prayer for himself on going abroad.[42]

In his report on his time in France, Boddy stated:

> I was stirred deeply as I affectionately pleaded for Christ to be their Helper in these days, and more than that, their life now and hereafter. 'Is there a clergyman here sir?' said a young soldier, 'I want to take Christ with me into the trenches'. I trust that the Holy Spirit will cause the message to bear fruit for eternity.[43]

Boddy further reported that the German Army were driven back at the Battle of the Marne. He attributed this victory to the prayers that were going up in Great Britain.[44]

In his article, 'The Vision at Mons', Boddy wrote, 'The Editor of *Confidence* has no doubt that the angel forms are being seen on the battlefield'.[45]

In *Confidence*, October 1915, Boddy published further evidence of the Angels of Mons.[46]

---

[39] *Confidence* 8.5 (May 1915), p. 91.
[40] *Confidence* 8.5 (May 1915), p. 93.
[41] *Confidence* 8.6 (June 1915), p. 107.
[42] *Confidence* 8.6 (June 1915), p. 109.
[43] *Confidence* 8.7 (July 1915), p. 129.
[44] *Confidence* 8.9 (Sept. 1915), p. 147.
[45] *Confidence* 8.9 (Sept. 1915), p. 167.
[46] *Confidence* 8.10 (Oct. 1915), pp. 191-93.

In one of his numerous reports, 'With the Troops in France', Boddy explained the position of the Chaplains:

> Church of England, Presbyterian, Free Church, Roman Catholic, and Jewish. They are all in the same uniform as the other officers, and have a rank as Captain, Major, Lieutenant-Colonel, etc., up to Chaplain-General.[47]

Boddy reported on 'A Parade Sermon' given by Major C.F. Kennedy, on the theme of, 'the wages of sin is death, but the gift of God is eternal life, through Jesus Christ our Lord'.[48]

In his long-running articles under the heading, 'With our Troops in France', Boddy reported on his meetings with soldier, Private H.E. White, a Pentecostal believer from Salisbury. Of him, Boddy wrote, 'Private White is doing his bit splendidly'.[49]

Writing of the death of a friend in the trenches, Sergeant William Ramshaw, Boddy suggested that he had, 'died for his country … he was beloved of all – a true practical Christian'.[50]

In his report on the National Convention at Westminster, 1916, Boddy wrote, 'Occasionally the meetings began with the singing of the "National Anthem", which nearly everyone sang with heart and voice. Sometimes there were earnest prayers for the country and for our lads in the trenches. Prayer was offered for our brethren abroad, now sadly departed from us.'[51] In the same report, Boddy wrote:

> On the Great Northern Railway I met two of the men of my son's battalion (18th Durham Light Infantry). They were delighted to meet Lieut'. Boddy's father. They were on their way back to France and bore some messages to him at the firing-line. God Bless them![52]

Boddy published his article, 'Evangelistic Work among Soldiers'. This was followed by 'The Last Message of a Christian Officer, killed in action on November 11th, 1916, and buried in France at Eaucourt l'Abbay'. Boddy included this officer's letter, which was

---

[47] *Confidence* 8.9 (Sept. 1915), p. 172.
[48] *Confidence* 8.9 (Sept. 1915), p. 172.
[49] *Confidence* 8.11 (Nov. 1915), p. 208.
[50] *Confidence* 8.11 (Nov. 1915), p. 209.
[51] *Confidence* 9.7 (July 1916), p. 111.
[52] *Confidence* 9.7 (July 1916), p. 112.

forwarded to his wife, by her husband's Colonel, following his death.[53]

Under 'Pentecostal Items', Boddy gave a brief account of his work as acting Chaplain to the men in their billets, this work included the supply and distribution of the Testaments of The Pocket Testament League. Boddy reported that in this work he had placed about 2000 Testaments into the hands of soldiers.[54]

Under the heading, 'The Editor's Son in France', Boddy wrote in order to update his readers on the health situation of his son, Lieut. J.A.V. Boddy, R.A.S., 'who, whilst on dangerous air duty in France, was shot down by hostile aeroplanes and badly "smashed"'.[55]

Boddy attempted to set the record straight regarding the story of the Angels, said to have appeared on the battlefield at Mons. The issue had been clouded by the controversy caused by the proven false witness of two soldiers. Boddy included a comment by Bishop Dr. Handley Moule, who suggested that the incident illustrated God's 'superhuman interposition in our [Britain's] favour'.[56]

Boddy, under the article heading, 'Forgiving and Forgiven', revisited the story of Nurse Edith Cavell; shot by German troops for helping Allied soldiers. He reflected upon her words:

> She was now facing eternity and she knew that patriotism was not enough. She must love everyone – 'Everyone', she said.[57]

In the July-September 1919 issue of *Confidence*, Boddy attempted to revive the theme of, 'Real Angels at Mons' with 'Some further corroborative facts'.[58] The War had ended some months before.

In the October-December 1919 issue of *Confidence*, Boddy, twice mentioned the story of Nurse Edith Cavell.[59]

Boddy reflected upon Pastor Paul and his family's losses during the Great War; he had lost two sons, and his wife died in 1919. He

---

[53] *Confidence* 10.1 (Jan-Feb. 1917), pp. 3-5.
[54] *Confidence* 10.3 (May-June 1917), p. 39.
[55] *Confidence* 11.2 (April-June 1918), p. 33.
[56] *Confidence* 11.2 (April-June 1918), pp. 21-22.
[57] *Confidence* 12.3 (July-Sept. 1919), p. 44.
[58] *Confidence* 12.3 (July-Sept. 1919), p. 49.
[59] *Confidence* 12.4 (Oct-Dec. 1919), pp. 56 and 63.

wrote, 'we deeply sympathise with our dear friend in the losses he has sustained'.[60]

Boddy published a note to the effect that copies of 'Real Angels at Mons' were available upon request from his Sunderland Vicarage.[61]

Boddy wrote under the heading: 'The Alleluia Victory' and included the story of how the English Army routed the Picts and Scots in the 4th Century, by shouting, 'Alleluia'.[62]

From 1921, Boddy's articles in *Confidence* became quite sparse. The size of each publication was also reduced substantially. The indexing of *Confidence* was also changed.[63]

In 1921, three years after the WWI ceasefire, Boddy included an article in *Confidence* entitled, 'Palestine Items', and went on to describe the exploits of Lord Allenby, who saved Jerusalem from bombardment through prayer.[64] Boddy then included a report on the event of Churchill's visit to Palestine.[65]

Boddy wrote an inspiring testimony of significant parts of his own life, under the heading, 'A Personal Testimony'.[66] In the section of *Confidence* entitled 'Personal Jottings', Boddy wrote with further news of his son.[67] He then told of his own move from All-Saints, Sunderland, where he had served for 38 years of ministry, to Pittington Hallgarth.[68]

In the last few years of *Confidence*, Boddy indicated that funds for its publication and distribution were running low.[69] *Confidence* was published in May 1925, and the last issue, No. 141, was published during 1926. Boddy as editor and publisher was its overseer from its inception, and first issue, in April 1908.

Chapter 5 gives a critical evaluation of Boddy's patriotism and addresses a number of the issues raised in this chapter.

---

[60] *Confidence* 13.1 (Jan-Mar. 1920), p. 12.
[61] *Confidence* 13.2 (April-June 1920), p. 27.
[62] *Confidence* 13.4 (Oct-Dec. 1920), p. 58.
[63] From the first 1921 edition, new indexing applied.
[64] *Confidence* 125 (April-June 1921), p. 21.
[65] *Confidence* 125 (April-June 1921), p. 22.
[66] *Confidence* 131 (Oct-Dec. 1922), pp. 52-53; 56-58.
[67] *Confidence* 132 (Jan-March 1923), p. 62.
[68] *Confidence* 132 (Jan-March 1923), pp. 63-67; 70-73.
[69] *Confidence* 139 (Nov-Dec. 1924), p. 150.

4

BOOTH-CLIBBORN'S PACIFISM

Booth-Clibborn's pacifism was based upon his understanding and experience of Christianity.[1] It was also influenced by his Quaker upbringing, and Quaker pacifist teaching. He well understood, and soon adopted, Quaker pacifist principles and worldview. His pacifism was also based upon his assessment of both Old and New Testament teaching and principles; upon an appeal to the events of early Church history and Christian practice, and also included an appeal to a number of historical figures. These aspects of Booth-Clibborns pacifism are each considered:

Kate wrote of her husband's ancestry:

> Commissioner Booth-Clibborn was of a long and distinguished Quaker ancestry which included such figures as Robert Barclay, the Quaker Theologian, and Elizabeth Fry, the prison philanthropist, as well as Anne Askew, the martyr.[2]

The contributions of these three individuals is briefly outlined: First, Robert Barclay, was born in northern Scotland in 1682, and was a well-respected theologian, writer, and politician. He wrote *Theses Theologiae,* in 1676, and later that year, published a work on Quaker faith and practice, *An Apology for the True Christian Divinity.*[3] Secondly, Elizabeth Fry, also a Quaker, worked tirelessly in the areas

---

[1] Booth-Clibborn, *Blood Against Blood,* p. 6.
[2] Booth, *A Poet of Praise,* p. 13.
[3] http://digitalcommons.robertbarclay.edu/grt/vol110/iss1/2 (accessed 1.9. 2016).

of prison, and social reform. Her life and work are celebrated in a number of places, for example: at the Friends Meeting House, Norwich – the city of her birth (1780), and in the Lady's Chapel at the Anglican Cathedral, Manchester.[4] Thirdly, Anne Askew was born in Grimsby, Humberside in 1521. She was an articulate protestant writer, preacher and activist, and an early convert to Reformed doctrine. She was charged with heresy in London in 1545. Askew refused to renounce her beliefs and was condemned as a heretic; she was then tortured on the rack at the tower of London, and later, martyred at Smithfield in 1546 – at the age of twenty-five.[5]

These three characters illustrated well the ancestry of Booth-Clibborn and were significant within both Quakerism, and wider Protestantism. His forbears were confident in their faith; they were prepared to stand their ground firmly for what they believed, irrespective of the cost to them personally, and their faith declaration was frequently in the public arena. Booth-Clibborn was also fearless in expressing his Christian faith, which he refused to divorce from pacifism.

Kate wrote further of her husband Booth-Clibborn and his association with Quakerism:

> Booth-Clibborn's ancestry fitted him … for the blood and fire of Salvationism and the Sword of the Spirit, because like all Quakers – like his own forbears who had destroyed their guns during the Irish Rebellion – he was an ardent pacifist.[6]

From the experiences of his own life, Booth-Clibborn wrote:

> Personally I owe much spiritually to a faithful Minister of the Society of Friends who, in his younger days, forced into service in the American civil war, refused to bear arms, was treated as demented, and went through several of the fiercest battles, that of Gettysburg among others, with a gun tied to his shoulder, doing all he could meanwhile for the wounded and the dying. He subsequently became a man of God of great power, and it was

---

[4] http://digitalcommons.elizabethfry.edu/grt/vol110/iss1/2 (accessed 1.9. 2016).

[5] Melanie Perry (ed.), 'Anne Askew', *Chambers Biographical Dictionary* (London: Chambers & Harrap, 1997), p. 91.

[6] Scott, *The Heavenly Witch*, p. 48.

under his ministry I received the baptism of the Holy Ghost[7] which led me to consecrate my own life to the war of redemption in its most extreme forms.[8]

Booth-Clibborn reflected upon the Quaker movement, and its pacifist history:

The Society of Friends [the Quakers] – that religious denomination which has for 250 years borne a testimony against war in the name of Christianity, against mere brute force as a means to spiritual ends.[9]

In 1660, George Fox and other Quaker leaders issued a clear declaration of nonviolence to Charles II. It outlined the Quaker (the Society of Friends) position:

We utterly deny all outward wars and strife and fightings with outward weapons, for any end or under any pretence whatsoever. And this is our testimony to the whole world. The spirit of Christ, by which we are guided, is not changeable, so as once to command us from a thing as evil and again to move unto it; and we do certainly know, and so testify to the world, that the Spirit of Christ, which leads us into all Truth, will never move us to fight and war against any man with outward weapons, neither for the Kingdom of Christ, nor for the kingdoms of this world.[10]

About one-hundred years before the time of Quakerism, the two-kingdom argument was used by the Mennonites in favour of pacifism. On this theme, Walter Klassen observed:

Basic to the Anabaptist view of government was their version of the two kingdoms doctrine. The kingdom of Christ was characterized by peace, forgiveness, nonviolence, and patience. The kingdom of this world, or Satan, was strife, vengeance, anger, and the sword which kills. Government belonged to the kingdom of the world ... A servant of Christ had no liberty to use

---

[7] The Holy Spirit in contemporary useage.

[8] Booth-Clibborn, *Blood Against Blood*, p. 21.

[9] Booth-Clibborn, *Blood Against Blood*, p. 41.

[10] Cherice Bock, 'Quakers on the Spectrum of Nonviolence: In Conversation with K. Barth, Reinhold Niebuhr, J.H. Yoder, M.L. King Jr., and Robert Barclay', *Quaker Religious Thought* 110.1/2, Article 2, 2008. < http:// digitalcommons.georgefox.edu/qrt/vol110/iss1/2 > (Accessed 1.9.2016).

coercion and vengeance or to kill because it was contrary to the commandments of Christ ...[11]

There is therefore no need for many words, for it is clear that Christians can neither go to war nor practise vengeance. Whosoever does this has forsaken and denied Christ, and Christ's nature.[12]

Looking back over the years of the peace witness, the historian, Donald Durnbaugh has suggested:

One could point to the peace witness of the Quakers, Brethren, and Mennonites, as one example. This unpopular stance has retained surprising vitality, for all the defections from it, in the face of continual and often massive societal pressure against it, and still waxes strong.[13]

Durnbaugh also observed that the Historic Peace Churches were the Mennonites, the Brethren, and the Quakers.[14] From his assessment of their history, he noted:

The Society of Friends has probably been the most articulate ... in protesting warfare and killing and suggesting alternative courses of conduct for governments. In the popular mind, Quakers are completely identified with pacifism.[15]

The Quakers and the Peace Churches, because of their pacifist principles, generally chose to oppose the State on the issue of war, on preparation for it, and participation in it. Booth-Clibborn held tenaciously to these principles throughout his life and ministry.

Martin Ceadel has outlined Christian pacifism from the perspectives of its aims and objectives:

Mainstream Christian pacifism ... derives its objection to fighting not from selected biblical texts, nor from the desire to avoid religious contamination, but from the incompatibility of

---

[11] Walter Klassen, *Anabaptism in Outline* (Ontario: Herald Press, 1981), pp. 244-45.

[12] Peter Riedman, *Account* 1542, in Klassen, *Anabaptism*, p. 278.

[13] Durnbaugh, *The Believers' Church*, p. 301, citing Otto Piper, *Protestantism in an Ecumenical Age* (Philadelphia: Fortress Press, 1965), p. 170.

[14] Durnbaugh, *The Believers' Church*, p. 225.

[15] Durnbaugh, *The Believers' Church*, p. 256.

all war with its perception of Christ's teaching as a whole ... its purpose is not to save the elect from sin, or even to save society from material disaster, but to redeem mankind through the power of Christian love.[16]

He further asserted:

The Quaker objection to war is well documented; it was based not on any explicit law against bearing arms or taking lives, but an intuitive and subjective interpretation of the 'inner light'. The inner light could easily be identified with what non-Quaker Christian's invoked with equal subjectivity, as the 'mind of Christ'.[17] Nothing is more important in that we should ask 'what is the teaching of Jesus?' Before we confuse the issue by going on to ask, 'is it practicable for us today to follow that teaching?'[18]

Although written some years after the time of Booth-Clibborn, Ceadel has here captured the ground of Booth-Clibborn's understanding of pacifism, and his objection to militarism and war.

John Stott, a leading Anglican, and pacifist in WWII, has expressed his views of Early Church history and the 'just war' position. The following quotations offer his insights into these themes:

It seems to be historically proven that for two centuries, until the conversion of Constantine, the great majority of Christians refused to serve as soldiers, as pacifists argued that they also perceived war to be incompatible with their Christian obedience.[19]

For a war to be classified as 'just': its cause must be righteous, defensive, and not aggressive; its means must be controlled with no unnecessary violence; and its outcome must be predictable.[20]

... ['just war'] was Christianized by Augustine in the fourth century, systematized by Thomas Aquinas in the thirteenth, further developed by Francisco de Vitoria in the sixteenth, and endorsed

---

[16] Martin Ceadel, *Pacifism in Britain 1914-1945: The Defining of a Faith* (Oxford: Clarendon Press, 1980), p. 21.

[17] Ceadel, *Pacifism in Britain*, p. 25.

[18] Ceadel, *Pacifism in Britain*, p. 206, citing, G.H.C. Macgregor, *The New Testament Basis of Pacifism* (London: James Clark, 1936) p. 7.

[19] John Stott, *Issues Facing Christians Today* (London: Marshall Pickering, 1990), p. 87.

[20] Stott, *Issues Facing Christians Today*, p. 87.

by most of the Reformers. It is held by a majority of Roman Catholics and Protestants today.[21]

The pacifist position was adopted by the so-called 'Radical Reformers' of the sixteenth century (the various Anabaptist groups), is preserved by the 'Peace Churches' today (Quakers, Mennonities, United Brethren, etc), and is held by considerable minorities in the 'historic' Reformation churches.[22]

Stott also observed:

The Society of Friends has probably done more in the field of general humanitarian effort proportionately than any other religious body.[23]

Stott's views here mirror the views of Booth-Clibborn – he had argued that the teaching of Jesus among Christians remained largely intact up to the time of Constantine.

Booth-Clibborn raised a number of additional issues: on 'just war', the work of the Holy Spirit, the blood and death of Jesus Christ, and his hope for the future, he states:

From Constantine, Paganism and Christianity became fused – or to change the simile; the Lamb lay down beside the Wolf … 'Christian war' with the sword began to be looked upon as normal and necessary.[24]

Christians must stand for the blood of Christ, 'once shed', and not attempt to stand for 'blood shedding'; it cannot be appropriate to stand for both.[25]

Power is only found in Pentecostal baptisms of fire, the exact opposite of the fiery baptisms of war.[26]

Christianity is the *only* remedy to war'.[27]

---

[21] Stott, *Issues Facing Christians Today*, p. 87.
[22] Stott, *Issues Facing Christians Today*, p. 87.
[23] Stott, *Issues Facing Christians Today*, p. 87.
[24] Booth-Clibborn, *Blood Against Blood*, pp. 49-50.
[25] Booth-Clibborn, *Blood Against Blood*, p. 29.
[26] Booth-Clibborn, *Blood Against Blood*, p. 23.
[27] Booth-Clibborn, *Blood Against Blood*, p. 45 (emphasis original).

Why should not every newly converted Christian be kept from the horrors of the past fifteen centuries, by being told from the first hour of his first love that the first Christians refused to bear arms and were right in doing so. This result can never be attained by studying any human standards of right and wrong, but by a careful painstaking study of the Scriptures. There we find 'the mind of Christ'.[28]

In these statements, Booth-Clibborn traces the context in which participation in war became 'normal and necessary' for Christians; the importance of an understanding of Christ's shed blood; the contrast between Pentecostal fire and warfare; Christianity as the remedy to war, and not least, the importance for Christians to adopt the mind of Christ, from conversion. He stressed the death of Christ, and the work of the Holy Spirit in a Christian's life, as inseparable from the pacifist position. He found that any attempt to separate these hallmarks of Christianity, was being unfaithful to the Christian Gospel. Commenting on the Ten Commandments, Booth-Clibborn asserted:

'Thou shalt not kill, thou shalt not steal, thou shalt not commit adultery, thou shalt not lie', are all one at the root, the first, second and fourth of these commandments are systematically broken in war.[29]

He outlined an example from Jesus' teaching:

Nothing can be clearer on this point than the words of our Lord. The terms He uses are always absolute and final. Darkness *or* light, life *or* death, truth *or* a lie, saving one's life *or* losing it – heaven *or* hell – and may we not now, as the summary of His life and teaching add – Salvation war [the work of the Christian church] or destruction war [militarism]. Between these extremes He recognised no middle course.[30]

Booth-Clibborn further asserted that in war:

Death and devastation are its normal goal, and you must go on, on, on to the bitter end, to the last smoking ruins of homesteads,

---

[28] Booth-Clibborn, *Blood Against Blood*, p. 67.
[29] Booth-Clibborn, *Blood Against Blood*, p. 71.
[30] Booth-Clibborn, *Blood Against Blood*, p. 71.

and the last charred remains of fathers, on, on to the last cruel climax.'[31]

In his book, *Blood against Blood*, Booth-Clibborn contrasts Christ's blood, as the blood shed once and for all, with the endless blood-shedding of war; both are gruesome; the blood 'from the pierced side of the Saviour on the cross', and the 'stream [that] bursts from a bayonet wound made in the breast of a Christian by a fellow-Christian'.[32]

Booth-Clibborn asserted a damning conclusion of the Christian Church:

> It is the fifteen centuries of awful 'Christian' wars for which he holds orthodox Christianity responsible. It has never dared to say war was wrong. On the contrary it has blessed the swords, the banners and the guns![33]

He further observed that Christian war is glorified in society and he referred to this as 'deluding'. On this theme he wrote:

> The inexpressibly awful realities of the distant battle-field are hidden from the eyes of English, French and German homes behind the gorgeous uniforms, the splendid music, the proud martial air of carnal superiority borne by masses moving with mathematical precision, accompanied by mighty mowing machines of death, provided by the highest Christian science of destruction. They pass by under gorgeous flags with double crosses upon them. On, on they move to the great harbours where floating in their sombre glory the awful Dreadnoughts [warships], and on and on across God's health-giving briny seas, on to the grim, gruesome climax. And meanwhile the officer occupies a superior position in the ball-room, and the highest national honour is heaped upon the returning conqueror. A place is kept for his tomb in St. Paul's or in Westminster Abbey.[34]

---

[31] Booth-Clibborn, *Blood Against Blood*, p. 75.

[32] Booth-Clibborn, *Blood Against Blood*, p. 44.

[33] Booth-Clibborn, *Blood Against Blood*, p. 48, citing a London City Temple pastor.

[34] Booth-Clibborn, *Blood Against Blood*, p. 51.

Booth-Clibborn stepped up his argument against 'Christian war' even further, when he wrote, that it is 'a ghastly crime against Christ'.[35] He affirmed that 'History, carnal and spiritual *always does* repeat itself',[36] and that is manifest in numerous wars. In these quotations, Booth-Clibborn provided a vivid description of the ways in which war was [and is] elevated within western culture. Because of his overtly pacifist views, his book, *Blood Against Blood*, was banned commensurate with military conscription, in 1916, in Britain. The book was first published in 1907 and revised in 1914.[37]

Reflecting upon the Boer War (1898-1901), Booth-Clibborn stated that 'the Salvationists [members of the Salvation Army] on both sides were bound by their very position to kill each other'. [38] From this statement, it is apparent that for Booth-Clibborn, pacifism is much more than a moral or ethical code; it is a life-principle and a closely-guarded worldview. Pacifism, for him, was not an optional extra; it was integral to his Christian life and faith.

Booth-Clibborn appealed to the opinions of historical figures, on the theme of war:

> John Wesley, 'Shall Christians assist the Prince of Hell, who was a murderer from the beginning, by telling the world of the benefit or the need for war?' George Fox, 'I cannot fight, for the spirit of war is slain within me'. Robert Barclay (1675), 'It is as easy to obscure the sun at midday, as to deny that the primitive Christians renounced all revenge and war.' General Sherman (USA), 'War is hell'. [39]

He further contrasted the claims of pacifism with a reflection upon the events of history and the narrative of John's Gospel:

> Napoleon so *loved* France that he *took* millions of her sons, and made them believe in him so utterly that whosoever among them

---

[35] Booth-Clibborn, *Blood Against Blood*, p. 52.

[36] Booth-Clibborn, *Blood Against Blood*, p. 53 (emphasis original).

[37] Both works are currently freely accessible at the British Library (as at January 2016).

[38] Booth-Clibborn, *Blood Against Blood*, p. 70.

[39] Booth-Clibborn, *Blood Against Blood*, pp. 109-10.

followed him to death might spread an endless amount of death through Europe.[40]

He continued:

> Whereas 'God *so loved* the world that He *gave* His only begotten Son, that whosoever believeth in Him should not perish, but have everlasting life' (John 3:16). Napoleon's wars cost eleven million lives, of which two million were of his own subjects.[41]

From this evaluation, it is seen that Booth-Clibborn included in his arguments here, an appeal to the wars of history, and their alarming statistics. He expressed his concern, that lies are obligatory in war.[42] Whilst on the subject of spying, he asserted that the whole process is built upon untruths, lying, and fabrication.[43] In support of his argument in favour of Christian pacifism, he further appealed to two thousand years of church history; in summary: to Justin Martyr, Tatian, Clemens of Alexandria, Tertullian, Cyprian, and others, they affirmed the unlawful nature of war, and the non-participation of early Christians. Origen, Ambrose, Chrysostom, Jerome and Cyril, gave also their opinions that it was unlawful for Christians to go to war.[44]

Booth-Clibborn, whilst being a prolific writer, and speaker, he took every opportunity to be a forthright apologist for Christian pacifism, within Quakerism, within the Salvation Army, during the period of his association with Alexander Dowie, and within early Pentecostalism in Britain.

The events of the Boer War provided the catalyst for Booth-Clibborn's book, *Blood Against Blood*, which articulated a clear defence of Christian pacifism. Whilst his pacifist views were taught to him during his early years in a Quaker family home, his responses to war were well developed by the time of The Boer War (1898-1901), and further by the events of the Great War.

A critical assessment of Booth-Clibborn's pacifism is given in Chapter 6.

---

[40] Booth-Clibborn, *Blood Against Blood*, p. 64 (emphasis original).
[41] Booth-Clibborn, *Blood Against Blood*, p. 64 (emphasis Booth-Clibborn's).
[42] Booth-Clibborn, *Blood Against Blood*, p. 101.
[43] Booth-Clibborn, *Blood Against Blood*, pp. 101-105.
[44] Booth-Clibborn, *Blood Against Blood*, p. 107.

5

A CRITICAL ASSESSMENT OF BODDY'S PATRIOTISM

In Chapter 3, elements of Boddy's patriotism were introduced. Included in this chapter is a critique and discussion of his patriotism. The opposing views of Booth-Clibborn and other writers are brought into the discussion.

Irrespective of one's own views of patriotism and pacifism, it is understandable that one might be uneasy in contemplating that an overtly Christian publication such as *Confidence* – 'A Pentecostal Paper for Great Britain', became a vehicle to promote patriotism, war, and militarism, at the outbreak of World War I, from 1914 onwards. Alexander Boddy, the publisher and editor of *Confidence* throughout the period of its publication (1908–1926), effectively took upon himself the task of war-correspondent from the outset of the war, and well beyond its conclusion. Gavin Wakefield, has summarised:

> *Confidence*, included numerous articles on travel, devotional, theological, news items, with 'some reflection on wider issues, notably including the Great War from its outbreak'.[1]

The term 'reflection' here seems over-generous, for as Allan Anderson has observed:

> *Confidence* soon became a strong defender of the 'just war' doctrine and published news on the progress of the allied troops and patriotic literature, including a statement by the Bishop of

---

[1] Wakefield, *Boddy*, p. 109.

Durham holding that this is a 'Holy War' against 'unprecedented peril of tyrannous domination of a single great state'.[2]

Donald Gee, when he reflected upon the years of the Great War, explained:

The First World War brought a surge of national patriotism, and as a State-Church clergyman A.A. Boddy was caught up in the tide.[3]

Boddy carefully avoided any detailed arguments of his own in support of the patriotic position, in the pages of *Confidence*. He preferred to publish the views of other patriots and was invariably dismissive of any views to the contrary.

Booth-Clibborn asserted that, 'war cannot be successfully performed without deception and lying in a hundred forms'.[4] Further, 'The power of the gospel message to the world and its authority upon [hu]mankind must have therefore been seriously reduced wherever Christian Churches or Associations have sanctioned war'.[5] From Booth-Clibborn's statements, it is clear that he believed that mixing the messages – in the case of *Confidence*, of Christianity and patriotism/militarism – had the potential to weaken the overall effectiveness of the gospel.

Writing his report on the 7th Sunderland Convention, in *Confidence* in June 1914, Booth-Clibborn seemed to sense the danger of what might be about to follow, when he proposed:

Feed on the Word. Reserve it to its supreme position. Let no literature, not even 'Pentecostal' usurp its place. Let no 'messages' become the source of 'leading'; let it be the Word, illuminated by the Spirit.[6]

Of Boddy's adventurous spirit, and his wish to instil this in his children: it is the right of every parent to help mould the lives of

---

[2] Allan Anderson, *Spreading Fires – The Missionary Nature of Early Pentecostalism* (London: SCM, 2007), p. 228, citing *Confidence* 7.9 (Sept. 1914), p. 163; 7.11 (Nov. 1914), pp. 203-208; and 8.1 (Jan. 1915), p. 5.

[3] Donald Gee, *These Men I Knew* (Nottingham: Assemblies of God Publishing, 1980), p. 22.

[4] Booth-Clibborn, *Blood Against Blood*, p. 14.

[5] Booth-Clibborn, *Blood Against Blood*, p. 15.

[6] *Confidence* 7.6 (June 1914), p. 104.

their children, but his later anguish over the near-death experiences of his son, finally his being shot down over France, perhaps should not have surprised him, for Boddy reported that his son 'has been in much active service on behalf of his country'.[7] Presumably this was with Boddy's blessing, if not his encouragement. Boddy's view of, and interest, in things military (as in the example of his family's boat trip to visit a war-ship moored offshore), would have been likely to leave lasting impressions upon his children.

There would have been those among Boddy's *Confidence* readership that might have reacted with surprise, or even disapproval, at his recourse to carrying a revolver and sturdy stick for the purpose of his self-defence and protection, when on his travels to North Africa, as detailed in his book *Kairwan*. Arguably, in this, Boddy could have been accused of not having sufficient faith or trust in God's promised presence, for his personal protection and safety when travelling. It also illustrates that he had no misgivings as to the use of a firearm, if he felt that this was needed.

Boddy's assertion that as an honorary chaplain during WWI, he was encouraging British soldiers in the camps, gave much scope for a pacifist response. Booth-Clibborn wrote on this theme:

> On the evangelistic work carried on among the soldiers by chaplains and others during the war some men are reported as having found Christ only a night or two before they were to die in battle. To bring men to the blood of Christ one day and cheer them on in a savage charge to shed the blood of fellow-men and fellow-Christians the next day! What term can qualify such a state of affairs? No word will fit the case. Words are either too strong or too weak, because the men were sincere. Therefore, we must go back to Calvary for the silent language of the pierced hands and feet.[8]

He then wrote further: 'Chaplains … who went among the soldiers … would possibly not receive their passes had they been known to preach that war was wrong',[9] and then reflected that 'they would not save men from war, so they sought to save them *in* war'.[10]

---

[7] *Confidence* 10.1 (Jan-March 1917), p. 7.
[8] Booth-Clibborn, *Blood Against Blood*, p. 75.
[9] Booth-Clibborn, *Blood Against Blood*, p. 76.
[10] Booth-Clibborn, *Blood Against Blood*, p. 76.

Boddy's decision to serve as Honorary Chaplain to the Allied Expeditionary Force, prompts a number of questions: did Boddy wish to evangelise the troops, bringing some to faith in Jesus Christ? Was his distribution of biblically-based tracts and New Testaments, in order to serve this purpose? Or, was it that he thought that such material would be of comfort or encouragement, as the soldiers carried them into the battle? Did Boddy fulfil his stated aim of encouraging the troops? Was this in the social setting, over teas and cakes, or was it in the religious services among groups of soldiers, that he was able to conduct? Keith Malcomson has suggested that Boddy went to France, 'where he ministered spiritually to the forces'.[11] The reports in *Confidence*, are not clear on these issues. Of Boddy's experiences as a chaplain, Boddy's daughter, Jane Vazeille Boddy, reflected:

> He was 60 when the War broke out and although over age, he persuaded the Chaplain General to allow him to go to France for a time, and although he never got farther than the base, he did good work among the soldiers.[12]

This serves to illustrate Boddy's persistence in his attempts to support patriotic goals.

On the theme of chaplaincy, Kevin C. Fielden wrote at length under the heading, 'Serving as Chaplains or Combatants?' He made a number of acute observations: the troops at the fighting front needed a sufficient number of chaplains; this was problematic to the Church, as many of its clergy were supportive of the war effort; the priority of the British Army was to transport its fighting men to the Western Front, rather than facilitating Anglican Chaplains to the Archbishop's satisfaction.[13] Fielden has suggested that 'many clergymen were convinced of the righteousness of the British cause'.[14] Many Anglican Church ministers actively encouraged recruitment to the armed forces. Archbishop Davidson in his letter

---

[11] Keith Malcomson, *Pentecostal Pioneers Remembered* (Longwood, USA: Xulon Press, 2008), p. 125.

[12] Boddy, Notes, p. 9.

[13] Kevin Christopher Fielden, 'The Church of England in the First World War', Electronic Theses and Dissertations, Paper 1080, 2005, p. 45. <http://dc.etsu/etd/1080> (Accessed 1.1.2015).

[14] Fielden, 'The Church of England', p. 42, citing Marrin, pp. 177-78.

published in Church Times, asserted that all households should send their men-folk to bear their part in the national war effort.[15] 'Anglican clergymen thought it both a duty and a privilege to aid the country throughout the War'.[16]

Boddy published numerous letters from soldiers in France, in order to bring their plight to the attention of his *Confidence* readership, and possibly also in order to endorse the patriotic position, stressing that some of these soldiers were Christians, including Pentecostal believers. He held the view that to be a soldier and a Christian was a good example of practical Christianity. Christian pacifists would have strongly disagreed with Boddy on this.

Whilst Boddy encouraged his *Confidence* readers on numerous occasions to pray for the soldiers, and for a British victory, this does prompt other questions; did Boddy believe that God was exclusively on the side of the British? And, would God choose to ignore the prayers of many thousands of believers in Germany?

On Boddy's friends in Germany, Pastor Paul, and others, Wakefield observed:

> When it came to the 1914-1918 war, he [Boddy] was a strong supporter of fighting against Germany, despite his many friendships with German pastors and considerable anguish over the matter. [17]

In *Confidence*, Boddy lamented these Christian friends in Germany, but went on to publish his own words, 'we will pray for victory!' He could not have envisaged the situation of Pastor Paul who lost two sons in the war; this would have been an unwelcome answer to Boddy's prayer for Pastor Paul.

Fielden observed that 'the concept of a Christian duty to fight was nearly universal among the Anglican clergy'.[18] He further asserted 'Marrin was unable to find a single man who had taken Anglican Orders who denounced the war for the reasons traditionally put forth by Christian pacifists'.[19] He adds, 'it is not surprising that these pastors would enthusiastically support the war from their

---

[15] Fielden, 'The Church of England', p. 43, citing Marrin, p. 180.
[16] Fielden, 'The Church of England', p. 30, citing Marrin, p. 186.
[17] Wakefield, *Boddy*, p. 123.
[18] Fielden, 'The Church of England', p. 33.
[19] Fielden, 'The Church of England', p. 33, citing Marrin, p. 147.

pulpits'.[20] The outspoken Bishop of London, Arthur Winnington-Ingram, 'claimed to have added ten thousand men to the armed services with his sermons and other recruiting'.[21] 'He called for the men of England to "band in a great crusade – we cannot deny it – to kill the Germans"'. Fielden further observed, 'it was seemingly appropriate to allow that Germans were in fact praying to God, their problem being that He was only listening to the British'.[22]

When Boddy published Polman's letter in *Confidence*, in which Polman reported visits to soldiers in Germany, Belgium, and England, he stated that the pacifists – Booth-Clibborn, George Jeffries, Dr. Phair, and others – had made their mission quite clear to the soldiers, in that they had nothing to do with the war effort, but had come to bring the Gospel of Jesus Christ. Boddy's response was to publish Scroggie's pro-war article in *Confidence*. In publishing this article, Boddy seemed to have placed his trust in a rather limited argument in favour of patriotism/militarism. On this theme, Booth-Clibborn had written, some years before:

> War is therefore like Christianity – an absolute system. To acknowledge war to be right in some cases is to give away the whole case and surrender the very citadel of Christianity. The very word patriotism, as used in war, is anti-Christian for it denies the brotherhood of man, and therefore denies the fatherhood of God. [23]

Booth-Clibborn equated war to theft, where life and land are stolen; both land and life belong ultimately, to God; the Old Testament Law 'thou shalt not steal' parallels with 'thou shalt not kill'. [24]

When in *Confidence*, Boddy discussed Booth-Clibborn's request to publish his new lyrics for the tune Tipperary, and also to recommend his book, *Blood Against Blood,* to the readers of *Confidence*; Boddy refuted Booth-Clibborn's lyrics, putting forward instead, lyrics of his own, which were intended for the use of 'soldiers and Christian men as they were marching'. Boddy also challenged the validity of Booth-Clibborn's book, and used the example put

---

[20] Fielden, 'The Church of England', p. 33.
[21] Fielden, 'The Church of England', p. 35.
[22] Fielden, 'The Church of England', p. 34.
[23] Booth-Clibborn, *Blood Against Blood*, p. 16.
[24] Booth-Clibborn, *Blood Against Blood*, p. 16.

forward in Scroggie's article against pacifism, whilst recommending Frank Ballard's pro-war book instead. This served to illustrate Boddy's rejection of the pacifist position. Boddy repeatedly published letters and articles from Christian soldiers, as if to portray that the pro-military position as the only position for his *Confidence* readers to adopt. Those were his views, and he promoted them whenever possible.

Booth-Clibborn suggested that the themes and idea of war are handed down:

> In all sincerity from generation to generation, without the slightest qualm of conscience, and with each succeeding decade the machinery with which humanity grinds up humanity grows more and more formidable, quick working and complete.[25]

He further warned: 'Christless theologies, or reformed religions, which have reformed Christ himself, are knocking loudly at the door'.[26] He clearly understood that such groups or movements diminish the teaching of Jesus, to such an extent that they no longer impinge upon how a believer lives or upon what they do.

When Boddy requested in the pages of *Confidence* (January 1915) that his American readers send in to him interesting articles about the war, he may not have been aware of the extent of Booth-Clibborns pacifist influence through his book, *Blood Against Blood*. If he was aware of it, then he chose to ignore it. The book had made a significant impact in North America. Such was the impact, that the Pentecostal group, Assemblies of God, USA, wrote Christian pacifism into their Constitution. On this, the American educator, pastor, pacifist, and writer, Paul N. Alexander, stated:

> Arthur Sydney Booth-Clibborn's book, *Blood Against Blood*, was reprinted in New York in 1914, by the publisher Charles Cook. The book was 'highly recommended' by the Pentecostal group, Assemblies of God, in the USA, to such an extent that the Christian pacifist position was incorporated within the General Council Combined Minutes, 1914-1917'.[27]

---

[25] Booth-Clibborn, *Blood Against Blood*, p. 90.
[26] Booth-Clibborn, *Blood Against Blood*, p. 48.
[27] Paul N. Alexander, 'Historical and Theological Origins of Assemblies of God', *Quaker Theology* 12.1 (2005-2006). quest@quaker.org (access-ed 1/6/2013).

The extent of the influence of Booth-Clibborn, was also acknowledged by Allan Anderson:

> Across the Atlantic, however, the AG [USA] enthusiastically endorsed the book as a 'most striking, realistic and forceful book' that presented 'war from a Christian standpoint'. Their Gospel Publishing House was the USA distributor for it, offering the book at a special price. It was widely publicised in other American Pentecostal periodicals'.[28]

And further:

> The Assemblies of God [USA] press recommended that its readers purchase it [Booth-Clibborn's book] and became imbued with the spirit of its content, in a complete opposition and protest against war and the shedding of blood.[29]

The result of this development may well have contributed towards Boddy's isolation as a patriot among a growing number of pacifists within early Pentecostalism, both in America, and in Britain.

Boddy, on many occasions, published articles in *Confidence* that added weight to his patriotic views. The Bishop of Durham's article, which asserted that the Great War was a Holy War; that we should pray for the fullest success; for the most decisive victory on the Allied side, and that Britain's hands were nobly white and clean. On this scenario, Booth-Clibborn had described such as: 'those who seek to combine the principles of Christianity with those of modern warfare'.[30] He asserted, a Christian soldier, 'is a soldier first and a Christian afterwards' … 'He must hate his fellow men for the love of "God and country"'.[31] Further, 'he must be systematically blinded to the good points of the nation he is to kill … he is a patriot above all else'.[32] Booth-Clibborn went on to assert that the question must be faced:

> Are these wars both Christian and anti-Christian, both wisdom and madness, both a blessing and a curse, both a kindness and a

---

[28] Anderson, *Spreading Fires*, p. 225.
[29] Anderson, *Spreading Fires*, p. 225.
[30] Booth-Clibborn, *Blood Against Blood*, p. 24.
[31] Booth-Clibborn, *Blood Against Blood*, p. 25.
[32] Booth-Clibborn, *Blood Against Blood*, p. 25.

cruelty, both divine and diabolical? Are they both a supreme good, in being the best means for advancing missionary effort among the heathen, and a supreme evil in spreading civilised sin, pride, vice, avarice, selfishness, in a thousand cultivated forms, and war with countless new types of massacreing machinery?'.[33]

When Boddy asserted that whilst God was on OUR[34] side, each one should ask, am I on God's side? He believed that God was on the side of the British expeditionary forces, but from his question; 'am I on God's side?' it is not clear whether Boddy doubted his own patriotism here, or whether he was challenging the pacifist case. The issues of patriotism and pacifism were of paramount importance to many Pentecostals in Britain at this time.

Boddy, in making the distinction between British heroes and German soldiers and officers, fell into the trap of using the polemics of war. Given Boddy's clearly expressed views on Christian love, unity, and spirituality, he appears, arguably, to have undermined his own stated beliefs and teaching, unless he felt that these could be placed on hold during war-time. Booth-Clibborn addressed such issues when he stated: 'It is not enough for the Christian to be anti-militarism, rather, "pro-Christian"'.[35] 'The present hour thus demands of Christians a solemn re-examination of their whole position, and a more complete return to the forces, *to all the forces* of primitive authentic Christianity.'[36]

Following the overtly pacifist convictions made clear in Voget's letter, Boddy reacted, by publishing a letter written by a Christian British Soldier, in which he described a soldier's view of war in the trenches.[37] Booth-Clibborn then answered this with an appeal to Church history:

> The early Christians *felt* war to be wrong, and new converts [to Christianity] do the same today. Not till they have been systematically misled and deceived by the semi-pagan sophistries [false

---

[33] Booth-Clibborn, *Blood Against Blood*, p. 27.
[34] Upper case letters appear in the original, quoted in Chapter 3 of this book.
[35] Booth Clibborn, *Blood Against Blood*, p. 125.
[36] Booth-Clibborn, *Blood Against Blood*, p. 134 (emphasis original).
[37] *Confidence* 7.10 (Oct. 1914), pp. 191-92.

arguments] which pass for Christian wisdom all around, not till then do they even begin to reconcile war with the gospel.[38]

In expressing these views, Booth-Clibborn risked alienating himself from Christians, such as Boddy, who held the view of 'just war'. However, Booth-Clibborn pursued this theme further:

> One of the first impulses of every new convert is to look upon war as wrong, and as contrary to the newly-born spirit of love and saving mercy within him. To get us to believe the contrary he has to be educated in the false philosophy of a low-level Christianity.[39]

Boddy, in summarizing his experiences as a chaplain in France, maintained the position of one who encouraged the troops in their endeavours. He saluted his brave fellow-countrymen who stood firm, and he asserted that God would give victory to individuals and nations. A response to this position is given in the words of Siegfried Sassoon, a captain on the Western Front in WWI:

> I am a soldier, convinced that I am writing on behalf of soldiers. I believe that this war, upon which I entered as a war of defence and liberation, has now become a war of aggression and conquest. I believe that the purposes for which I and my fellow soldiers entered upon this war should have been so clearly stated as to make it impossible to change them, and that, had this been done, the objects which actuated us would now be attainable by negotiation. I have seen and endured the suffering of the troops, and I can no longer be a party to prolong these sufferings for ends which I believe to be evil and unjust.[40]

In this recorded instance, the grim realities of war are at serious odds with the ideals of its justification.

Boddy's published letter from Captain Ball described how he had put fifty hostile planes out of action. In the letter sent to his mother, he laments that whilst he is looked after by God, he is tired of living

---

[38] Booth-Clibborn, *Blood Against Blood*, p. 59 (emphasis original).

[39] Booth-Clibborn, *Blood Against Blood*, p. 58.

[40] Dan Todman, *The Great War – Myth and Memory* (London: Hambledon Continuum, 2005), p. 128, citing J.M. Wilson, *Siegfried Sassoon: The Making of a War Poet 1886-1918* (London, 1998), pp. 373-74.

to kill, and will be pleased when he has finished. Boddy may not have realised it, but Captain Ball's letter, was really expressing a view that to be tired of killing and having a wish to stop what he was doing, would be the starting point of pacifist thinking for many at this time.

The issue of Sir Edward Grey, who was called a hypocrite by the German Press, troubled Boddy. He denounced this as an injustice. Boddy was perhaps naive in his expectations of what is normal behaviour on both sides in the events of war. On this, Booth-Clibborn had written, bringing into focus a number of arguments to demonstrate the insanity of war:

In war all things are inverted. Many a vice become a virtue. Lying and spying is part of the

patriotic work for which Christian governments secretly pay great sums of money to individuals of other nations, while ready to shoot individuals of their own nationality for similar services rendered to the 'enemy'.[41]

When Boddy published a letter sent to him from the USA, on the subject of the sin of intemperance, one wonders whether he believed its sentiments: that unless the sin of intemperance 'is put away from us', then God will not give us the victory. To Boddy temperance, and indeed membership of the Temperance Society, were serious issues and a major cause that he supported throughout his ministry. It is difficult to understand how one might give such prominence to this issue, to such an extent that the outcome of the war impinged upon it. On this, Fielden observed: 'to many Church leaders one of the most pressing social and spiritual issues of the day was that of drink',[42] but, 'the horror and loss of the war effort caused intemperance to pale in importance'.[43] One might speculate as to whether Boddy viewed the evil of drink, which he opposed, a greater evil than the War, which he wholeheartedly supported?

Mary Boddy, in her article, published in *Confidence*, under the heading, 'the War', proposed that war equates with sin. The article however, stopped short of a call to reject sin in all its forms. It is

---

[41] Booth-Clibborn, *Blood Against Blood*, p. 12.
[42] Fielden, 'The Church of England', p. 31.
[43] Fielden, 'The Church of England', p. 32.

unlikely that Alexander Boddy, Mary's husband, the editor of *Confidence*, would have allowed her to draw such a conclusion, even though her article could be interpreted in this way. In another article published in *Confidence*, Boddy asserted that in this war, the whole nation seems uplifted; the Colonies have rallied in support of an Empire; this will bring freedom – not militarism. There is much evidence to suggest that whilst Boddy may have sincerely believed this to be the case; the realities were in sharp contrast. Nick Lloyd has proposed that in WWI: '10 million soldiers died. Perhaps another 20 million others were scarred'.[44] Those scars were physical, mental, spiritual, personal, and social.

Boddy published in *Confidence* a declaration by the English Bishops which stated that the Great War was a just cause. Wakefield has observed that Boddy did not generally consult with others on issues of importance. For example, on the issue of racial tensions, he wrote:

> Boddy's own comments tended to assume the rightness of his own position, without his feeling any need to provide biblical or theological arguments in its favour.[45]

This also appears to be the case with his patriotic/militarist position. Perhaps in this area he was not secure enough to take on, by serious dialogue or argument, pacifists of the stature of Booth-Clibborn or Frank Bartleman, the outspoken American pacifist, speaker, writer, and visitor to England at this time. Boddy presumably felt more secure in his own views, when they were reiterated by the English Bishops.

Boddy asserted that in this War, we believe that God is on our side. In the same issue of *Confidence*, he included a letter from G. R. Polman of Amsterdam in which Polman asserted that they were looking at the War, not from a national standpoint, but from God's standpoint. Polman had been a Salvation Army worker under A.S. Booth-Clibborn, and was no doubt influenced towards pacifist faith by him.

---

[44] Nick Lloyd, *Hundred Days, The End of the Great War* (London: Penguin/ Viking, 2013), p. 271.
[45] Wakefield, *Boddy*, p. 150.

In Boddy's report on the London Convention of 1915, he urged Pentecostal people to pray down on our soldiers' and sailors' salvation in this cruel time of conflict. His comments are ambiguous in that he does not state whether he means salvation, as in repentance, grace, and faith, or salvation in the sense of the cessation of the War – he may have meant both.

When Boddy had concluded his tour as chaplain in France, his report included a soldier's comment, 'is there a clergyman here sir? I want to take Christ with me into the trenches.' In this situation, Boddy prays that Christ will be the soldier's helper. This in reality prompted serious theological and practical questions: will Jesus Christ be with the soldier in the trenches? Will he help him? This has to be answered with Jesus' specific command in mind (Mt. 5.38-46; Lk. 6.27-35).

Booth-Clibborn provided a response to this type of situation, when he reflected upon the words of a newly-converted soldier's testimony. The soldier had returned from fighting in the Boer War, and was then interviewed by Booth-Clibborn, who recorded:

> He told us with sobs of the horrors he had perpetrated in war. They were too awful for words:

> Pillage was legalised; outrage and rape accompanied it as a matter of course; his own hand had assassinated resisting victims; brandy, mixed with gunpowder, was drunk systematically, to give the required degree of madness, savage courage, and fiendish heartlessness.[46]

As recent events (i.e. the Chilcot Report on the Iraq War) have illustrated,[47] the whole process of attempting to justify war, may prove a difficult, if not futile, endeavour.

Boddy reported in *Confidence* that the German Army were driven back at the Battle of the Marne, due to the prayers going up in Great Britain. This view, of course, failed to recognise any validity in the prayers going up in Germany.

Boddy repeatedly raised the issue of the Angel of Mons. His belief in these events prompt the thought that this really somehow proved that in this 'spiritual' War, God must have been on the side

---

[46] Booth-Clibborn, *Blood Against Blood*, p. 22.
[47] The Iraq War, subject of the Chilcot Report, July 2016.

of the Allied Armies, exclusively. This issue was at the time clouded in controversy when two soldiers admitted that they had given false evidence. Boddy, in order to reinforce his position on this issue, included comments by Bishop Handley Moule, to the effect that God had intervened superhumanly in our [Britain's] favour.

In one of his numerous reports under the heading, 'With the Troops in France', Boddy explained the ranks of the Chaplains in relation to their military peers. Boddy seemed to be impressed with rank and order, but irrespective of title or rank, the chaplains were under the strict control of the military commanders. They did precisely what they were instructed to do.

Boddy's report on 'A Parade Sermon' given by Major C.F. Kennedy, on the theme of, 'the wages of sin is death, but the gift of God is eternal life through Jesus Christ our Lord'. This seems strangely out of place within the context of the Great War, and must have left many of those listening confused, in view of the fate that awaited the majority of them.

Boddy gave his patriotic endorsement of two soldiers, White, and Ramshaw, the latter he described as a true practical Christian. Comments of this type were destined to stir up pacifist disapproval within the early Pentecostal movement. On this issue, Booth-Clibborn recognised the plight of sincere Christians caught up in war. He wrote:

> No greater calamity can befall any sincere conscientious Christian than to be placed under two contradictory sets of laws at the same time, the one normal and the other abnormal, the one divine, and the other of man's invention with merely national ends.[48]

In view of this, he further suggested that it is appropriate to, 'remember how small, how trifling in the sight of God are the Empires of this world'.[49]

In his report on the London Convention of 1916, Boddy notes that the National Anthem was sung; prayers were also said for the country and for 'our lads in the trenches'. In this report, Boddy also mentions that he met two men from his son's battalion whilst

---

[48] Booth-Clibborn, *Blood Against Blood*, p. 73.
[49] Booth-Clibborn, *Blood Against Blood*, p. 74.

travelling. They were able to take messages from Boddy to his son at the forefront of the battlefield. From around this time, Boddy periodically included updates on his son's health in the pages of *Confidence*.

In France, Boddy worked tirelessly in the supply and distribution of Testaments of the Pocket Testament League. Boddy had great enthusiasm for this work and reported that he was able to place 2,000 Testaments into the hands of soldiers.

In several issues of *Confidence*, Boddy referred to the death of Nurse Edith Cavell. She was shot by German troops for helping Allied soldiers. Boddy reported on Cavell's well-known view, that we must love everyone, but he did not mention that Cavell would have also included those who took her life.

In the years following the Great War, Boddy continued to devote column space in each issue of *Confidence* relating repetitively to the theme of war. The incidents of the death of Nurse Edith Cavell, the Angel of the Mons, news of the health of his son, and so on, were featured. Almost a year after the War had ended; Boddy published the story of how the English Army routed the Picts and Scots in the 4th Century, by shouting, 'Allelujah'. The exploits of Lord Allenby were featured in *Confidence*, as late as 1922. Boddy obviously felt the need to perpetuate the themes of war, long after the Great War had ended.

When Mrs Wilshaw, of Leeds, submitted her report on the Amsterdam Conference of 1921, published in *Confidence*, she wrote that every trace of the war spirit and race prejudice was obliterated, among the delegates. It is possible that her carefully worded report was directed towards Boddy, and also to those *Confidence* readers who shared his patriotic views.

Boddy faithfully served the church in ministry at All-Saints, Sunderland, for a period of 38 years, and a further 8 years at Pittington Hallgarth; he was a respected pastor, who, in his mature years, majored on love, spiritual gifts, and unity among believers, but, arguably, he failed to come to terms with the patriotic-pacifist divide that he had helped create, and maintain within early Pentecostalism.

His unquestioning, poorly argued, patriotic position, appeared to have reached a disproportionate level of enthusiasm in his life, as he repeatedly attempted to keep the issues of war in front of his

Confidence readers, as if in an attempt to justify patriotism and militarism.

Boddy, like many of his Anglican peers at this time, failed to recognise the fact that ordained ministers within established Church groups, were exempt from military service, not least because it was felt by successive government authorities, that their position and social standing were incompatible with participation in warfare.

In other areas, for example on leadership, spiritual sifts, Christian unity, Boddy was unequivocal, and prescriptive. His *Confidence* readers were generally left in no doubt as to how they should apply his teaching; whereas in the area of patriotism, war, and militarism, it appeared that Boddy was able to divorce this area from all of his other views, as if in a vacuum, arguably untouched by his own teaching on: love, ethics, unity, and fellowship.

Bruce Milne has summarized the mood within evangelical churches in Britain at around this time:

> Among evangelicals, however, there was a great resurgence of interest in last things. Millennial views were championed and the hope of the Lord's imminent return burned strongly. All this had considerable influence in promoting the great nineteenth-century missionary and evangelistic endeavours, as well as evangelical concern for social improvement.[50]

Within early Pentecostalism in Britain, many believed that they were living in End Times, Boddy was no exception for he believed the Great War would soon result in the climax of the ages. He published a number of articles in *Confidence* to that effect. Boddy's patriotic position was in part influenced by this view, and whilst many agreed with Boddy's eschatology, for many others, the endorsement of militarism and war was a step too far.

Boddy's legacy is discussed in Chapter 8.

---

[50] Bruce Milne, *Know the Truth* (Leicester: IVP, 1982), p. 280.

6

A CRITICAL ASSESSMENT OF BOOTH-CLIBBORN'S PACIFISM

The nature of Arthur Sydney Booth-Clibborn's pacifism, outlined in Chapter 4, raises a number of issues that this chapter will assess critically. It is appropriate first to assess aspects of his character and personality.

His education, training, and development were effective in producing a learned, well-informed, and influential man of integrity and conscience. His linguistic and communication skills were put to good use as a speaker, translator, and writer: he could speak four languages fluently, and he wrote/composed more than 300 hymns. In France, he worked tirelessly to translate and publish the Salvation Army's French *War Cry*. His book, *Blood against Blood*, proved influential in Britain in causing young men to question military service. The book was banned by the Government in Britain, when conscription was enforced in 1916.

Booth-Clibborn also proved himself to be fearless: he managed 1,100 men and their machines at his father's linen mills. During this period, he was appointed a minister of the Society of Friends (the Quakers), while in his early twenties. Soon after this, he was appointed by General William Booth to serve as a missionary/evangelist in mainland Europe, where he suffered much hostility. Booth-Clibborn, however, valued the principles of personal pacifist faith and the call of God upon his life; he considered these of greater importance than the opinions of those who tried verbally or physically to attack him, his values, and his worldview.

Considering now, aspects of Booth-Clibborn's Christian pacifism: in defending his position, Booth-Clibborn appealed to his
Christian faith, to the Bible – both the Old and New Testaments,
to Church history, and to a number of key historical figures including the Church Fathers. He also asserted that his pacifism was
linked with his Quaker ancestry and his upbringing in a family committed to the pacifist tradition and its values.

Booth-Clibborn was exposed to the principles of pacifism from
an early age. For the majority of Quakers, strife, fighting, militarism
and war, preparations for war, and participation in it, were incompatible with the 'mind of Christ', and were contrary to his teaching.
This teaching was instilled early in the life of Booth-Clibborn, and
soon became integral to his thinking, and worldview. His life-long
faith, ministry, and writing were also a consistent witness to his pacifist faith.

A friend of Booth-Clibborn, a faithful Quaker minister who suffered greatly in war-time for his pacifist faith, was influential in
shaping Booth-Clibborn's life. This friend motivated Booth-Clibborn to devote his life to what he called 'the war of redemption',
the fight of the Christian faith; which for him, excluded all forms
of militarism and warfare.

Booth-Clibborn's comment that humans are at times unwilling
to receive any light on the subject of war; he found that many Christians were not easily convinced. This could suggest a bias in the way
that history has been taught in our schools. I recall, for example,
being taught about the numerous wars of British history, having to
memorise related dates and places; Britain usually featured among
the 'winners', rather than 'losers'. I also recall that little attention
seemed to be given to the casualties and costs of war, in terms of
the physical, mental, and spiritual scars that were made upon both
the immediate and future generations. Booth-Clibborn fully understood the horrors of war. On this scenario, Joseph Fahey has made
the following observations:

World War I was a new type of conflict in the tattered history
of humankind. In 1917, Marshal Foch of France pointed to this
when he stated: 'Truly a new era has begun, that of national wars
which are to absorb into the struggle all the resources of the
nation; which are not to be aimed at dynastic interests, but at the

defence or spread of philosophic ideas first, of independence and unity.' Nine million people were killed in World War I and the war neither ended war or made the world safe for democracy. Incompetence and outright stupidity characterised many of the decisions made by Prime Ministers and commanding officers on all sides. Soldiers became pacifists in the trenches, engaged in large and small mutinies, and even fraternised with the enemy, for example during the Christmas truces of 1914 and 1915. Yet the voice of the combat soldier was not heard until after the war ended.[1]

It is only now, from the perspective of the history of the past hundred years or so, that the words of Fahey begin to resonate with many who dislike militarism and war, and feel that it leaves its wounds and scars in so many areas: moral, ethical, financial, material, physical, mental, and spiritual, often solving little.

Donald Durnbaugh, in his observations of the Quaker (Brethren and Mennonite), peace witness, referred to it as an unpopular stance, but one of surprising vitality, even though societal pressure is massively against it, it still waxes strong. Booth-Clibborn, throughout his life, demonstrated his tenacity for the peace witness and testimony, even though, at times, the odds were stacked against him, for reasons of indifference, contrary views, or unbelief.

In *Blood Against Blood,* Booth-Clibborn was careful to point out that his pacifism was not a position that he took simply because his views were against war, but rather that his views were 'pro-Christian'.[2] He was unable to separate his pacifism from his personal belief in Jesus Christ – his teaching, and his ethics. Booth-Clibborn argued that Christ's overt teaching on the love of one's enemies had been lost to Christianity over the centuries. He asserted that the Christian Church, had failed to speak out against numerous wars. This denial had weakened the Church's message overall; for this reason, Booth-Clibborn's *Blood Against Blood* was predominantly centred around the theme of 'Christian war', and the biblical, pacifist response to this mind-set, and worldview. In addition to Jesus' own teaching, Paul the Apostle, in his teaching states that God's

---

[1] Joseph F. Fahey, *Peace, War, and the Christian Conscience* (London: Pax Christi UK, 2003), p. 10.
[2] Booth-Clibborn, *Blood Against Blood*, p. 125.

kingdom is comprised of: 'righteousness, and peace, and joy, in the Holy Spirit' (Rom. 14.17). The Fruit of the Spirit are also outlined by Paul as: love, joy, peace, longsuffering, gentleness, goodness, faith, meekness, and temperance (Gal. 6.22-24).

Booth-Clibborn, appealed to the pacifist witness of the Early Church, evident up to the time of Emperor Constantine (c. 274-337 CE). Constantine had decreed that Christianity be made the state religion of the Roman Empire in 326 CE. Up to that time, a great majority of Christians refused to serve as soldiers, under a succession of emperors. From about this time, Paganism and Christianity became fused, and the pacifist, non-violent aspects of Christianity's message began to fade, as militarism began to be looked upon as necessary and normal,[3] at least, up to the time of the radical reformers, including the Mennonites, in Europe, and later, in the USA.

Booth-Clibborn expressed his deep regret that in war, Christians might be found killing other Christians. In the Boer War, for example, he knew members of the Salvation Army who killed each other, being on opposing sides. This was also the case in World War I. For Booth-Clibborn, this state of affairs could never be right. He appealed to Christians to stand for the blood of Christ, 'once shed', and not attempt to stand for 'blood-shedding' as it is not appropriate to stand for both.

Booth-Clibborn believed that Christianity was the only remedy for war, but the reality, however, is complex. Joseph Fahey on this has written:

> World War I was a stern challenge to religion. Christian nations fought bitterly against each other. Historian Roland Bainton observed that 'the Churches in every land gave support to their governments'. In Germany, Catholics and Protestants alike looked upon the conflict as one of defence against enemies on the Fatherland's strangulation. In Britain and the United States, people of all faiths were united in support of war as never before.[4]

---

[3] See Stott, cited in Chapter 5.
[4] Fahey, *Peace, War, and the Christian Conscience*, p. 10.

In this scenario, depicted by Fahey, relatively few individuals launched any serious challenge to the call to arms.

Augustine's proposal that monks and ministers be exempt from participation in war was finally adopted, and this effectively weakened any obligation on their part to preach and teach pacifism in the churches. Many ordained ministers within church denominations or groups recognised by government authorities, are generally exempt from military service and have felt little obligation to preach or teach pacifism within their churches. This situation somewhat undermines Booth-Clibborn's view that Christianity is the only remedy for war. For this to be true, it must be received by its ministers, communicated to the church, then believed, and finally applied in lives. Due to the wide acceptance within the Protestant churches of the 'just war' position, military service has been viewed as an option, on the basis of the personal conscience of the Christian believer. Pacifists might argue that by failing to give guidance on this issue, many church leaders have neglected their primary role as a shepherd tasked with leading their flock.

The situation of Christianity universally accepting pacifism however is unlikely to materialise, as many 'Bible-believing' churches seem to be against pacifism, believing instead that the Christian's first duty is loyalty to the government. The fact that so many governments around the world seem to ignore the biblical principles of honesty, integrity, and justice, in their dealings with their own citizens or those of other countries, does not appear to feature in this thinking. Some churches also appear to reject contemporary biblical scholarship, as this is outside of their comfort zone. In this case, the approach of Booth-Clibborn, in his systematic evaluation of Christian pacifism, based upon an appeal to the Scriptures, to Church and social history, somehow would fail to appeal to their intellect or instinct. They continue to believe what they have always believed, and if that tradition does not include pacifism, they will continue to ignore it in perpetuity.

Some Christians, on the basis of a reading of the Apostle Paul's teaching, take the view that it is always appropriate to obey the laws of civil governments, and that includes when called to take up arms in military service. Paul, however, refers to Jesus as Lord, which put him at great risk of reprisals from the Roman authorities. Paul also asserted that the weapons of the Christian's warfare are spiritual rather than carnal – or man-made. Perhaps the clearest answer comes from the teaching of Jesus, when he was cornered into giving his thoughts on the issue of whether it was appropriate to pay taxes to Ceasar (Mt. 22.15-22; cf. Mk 12.13-17; Lk. 20.20-26). For Jesus to agree in the affirmative, would have meant rejection by his followers; alternatively, to oppose paying taxes would have meant likely arrest by the Roman authorities. In his answer to this question, Jesus called for a Roman silver coin, the *denarius*. When this was brought to him, he questioned them as to whose head and title were on the coin? When those listening affirmed that it was the emperor's head and title that was on the coin, Jesus suggested that they should give to the emperor the things that belonged to him, and to God, the things that are God's. Inscribed on the *denarius* was a portrait of the emperor, and the title, 'Son of God'. A patriotic Jew would not have carried this coin on their person,[5] as this would have signified a betrayal. This incident serves to illustrate the tensions that existed between Jesus' teaching on the Kingdom of God, and the kingdoms of this world. It also affirms that Jesus' followers are to be citizens of God's Kingdom and have allegiance to it. Alan Cole has commented, 'We cannot worship person, party, or state, but only God himself'.[6]

Philip Jensen has also commented on this theme:

> The coming of Christ has transformed key elements of the identity of the people of God. They are no longer defined by race or by land, but by faith in Jesus Christ. The radical change in dispensation following Easter remains that there is no warrant for applying the nationalistic aspects of the Old Testament, including the Yahweh war to the church.[7]

In his commentary on Rom. 13.1-7, in which he outlines the Christian's responsibility to government, Douglas J. Moo wrote:

---

[5] R.T. France, 'Matthew', in D.A. Carson *et al.* (eds.), *New Bible Commentary* (IVP: Leicester, 1994), p. 933.

[6] Alan Cole, 'Mark' in D.A. Carson *et al.* (eds.), *New Bible Commentary* (IVP: Leicester, 1994), p. 969.

[7] Philip Jenson, *The Problem of War in the Old Testament* (Cambridge: Grove Books, 2010), p. 26.

… the apparently absolute command to do what rulers tell us to do creates problems for most Christians. These problems are created not only by our experience – many believers must live under dictatorial and rabidly anti-Christian governments – but by the New Testament itself, which elsewhere hold up disobedience to some rulers as commendable (Acts 4:19-20).[8]

Moo added:

Paul's demand that Christians *submit* to government means simply that they recognize governments rightful place within the hierarchy of relationships established by God, a hierarchy at whose pinnacle is God. When, therefore, government usurps its place, and commands us to do something contrary to our ultimate Lord, we are free – indeed obliged – to disobey![9]

Moo further acknowledged that:

This view may weaken the meaning of 'submit'; perhaps the best solution, then, is to view Romans 13:1-7, as a general statement about how the Christian should relate to government, with exceptions to this advice assumed but not spelled out here.[10]

Booth-Clibborn's appeal is to the experience and practice of the Early Church – a view endorsed by John Stott – up to the time of Constantine, when Christians generally refused to serve as soldiers in the armies of successive Roman emperors. This contributed to their persecution, across the empire. The Early Church believers made every attempt to follow, and to be faithful to Jesus' teaching.

In contemporary Church life, where so many pastors/leaders repeatedly reflect upon the days of the Early Church, with appeals for a return to those days where God's Spirit moved with miraculous and prophetic power through the Apostles, particularly as it was in the times of Peter and Paul, as recorded in the Book of Acts. In such appeals, pacifism is generally excluded, as if it never really existed, and any appeal for non-violence, justice and peace, has, with few exceptions, been lost.

---

[8] Donald J. Moo, 'Romans' in D.A. Carson *et al.* (eds.), *New Bible Commentary 21st Century Edition* (Leicester: IVP, 1994), p. 1153.

[9] Moo, *New Bible Commentary*. p. 1153.

[10] Moo, *New Bible Commentary*. p. 1153.

Booth-Clibborn asserted that the Ten Commandments are systematically broken in war: he included killing, stealing, and lies. The explicit teaching of Jesus is also ignored in war. Booth-Clibborn further argued that death and destruction are the normal goals of war. Once started, war becomes difficult to stop; on it goes to its end of death and destruction. Numerous wars around the world in modern times seem to prove Booth-Clibborn's point.

Booth-Clibborn rejected any notion that wars might be classified as 'just'. He argued that the Church has adopted this position almost universally. From the time of Constantine, the common arguments as to the 'rightness' and 'justness' of war were promoted to such an extent, that support for the state, including in times of war, became almost inevitable for Christians, with few exceptions.

When Booth-Clibborn asserted that war is glorified in Western society and culture, he provided a vivid account of how war is glorified: with music, pageantry, and with the highest national honours 'heaped upon the returning conqueror'. He referred to this as deluding.

In modern society, some go to great lengths of effort and expense to promote modern warfare, in numerous books, films, and popular video games for young people. Much effort goes into Remembrance Days, in keeping the memory of the country's war dead alive, and this is understandable given the scale of death in the numerous wars of the past hundred or so years. It is right, irrespective of one's personal views of war, that the millions of families, relatives, and friends, who have suffered loss in this way are allowed time and space to remember and reflect. It does, however, remain a major puzzle that whilst many nations around the world remember the casualties of war, repeatedly, the process of remembrance, generally fails, as it never seems to enter the realm of understanding and learning. Humankind makes the same mistakes, engaging in war, repeatedly. National and local memorials to our war dead continue to tell the tragic story of almost unending wars. On this, Booth-Clibborn lamented that history always does repeat itself. Many state-church buildings reflect war and its remembrance, often with patriotic undertones, such as the positioning of flags and statues of armed soldiers. Whilst this may be of great comfort to those who are war-bereaved, it may be unhelpful to young people who might draw a conclusion that war, by being honoured in this way, is acceptable, normal, and always justifiable.

Booth-Clibborn appealed to a number of key historical figures in support of his pacifist position: John Wesley, George Fox, and Robert Barclay, all spoke out against war; General Sherman described war as 'hell'.

Booth-Clibborn parallels the wars of Napoleon with John's Gospel 3.16; he contrasted God's work of salvation with the horror of war and its grim statistics. He goes on to appeal to the opinions of the Church Fathers. Justin Martyr, Clement of Alexandria, Tertullian, Cyprian, Origen, Ambrose, Chrysostom, Jerome and Cyril, all endorsed a pacifist, non-violent position for Christians. It is clear that Booth-Clibborn made every effort to align his views with those who had been of significant influence throughout Christian history.

Booth-Clibborn's legacy is discussed in Chapter 8.

7

QUAKERISM AND EARLY PENTECOSTALISM IN BRITAIN[1]

This Chapter briefly outlines the social, political, and religious context of early Quakerism in Britain, the ministry of George Fox (1624-1691), his legacy, and parallels that exist between Quakerism and early Pentecostalism in Britain. It also outlines the distinctive nature of Quaker faith and practice, and examines why these 'non-negotiables', as he called them, were so important to Booth-Clibborn, in his life and ministry.

The term 'Quaker' in the seventeenth century was used in a derogatory manner and was intended to be offensive. The name was derived from the experience of some believers when they attended Quaker meetings in which God's Spirit was evident. They would quake or shake because of God's presence upon them.[2] Quakers were well known for their anticlerical views, and for their refusal to swear oaths and to pay tithes to the established church. This led to accusations of disloyalty to both Church and State and caused them to suffer vicious persecution. When the Quakers refused to pay their dues, their goods were often destroyed and their personal liberties curtailed.[3] They often despaired that they could not win,

---

[1] This chapter includes extracts from two articles by the same author: G. Craven, 'George Fox, Quaker leader, Man of the Spirit', *JEPTA*, 19.1 (2009), pp. 56-71, and in a shorter, popular version of the same article in: 'Drawn to the Father's Son', *Heroes of the Faith* 12.4 (Oct-Dec. 2012), pp. 14-17.

[2] J. Gardner and N. Wenborn (eds.), *History Today Companion to British History* (London: Collins & Brown, 1995), p. 592.

[3] Gardner and Wenborn, *History Today Companion to British History*, p. 39.

hounded as they were by their persecutors. A key factor in Quaker persecution was their pacifism. Their Declaration of 1660 stated simply that Christ's Spirit being unchangeable, would never move them to fight, bear arms, or go to war against another.[4] And, further, that the Spirit of Christ destroys the ground of enmity in humanity.[5] Not only did the Quakers promote peace, they also forgave those of their numbers who bore arms. This was a rare sentiment among radical groups.[6]

Like the pacifist Anabaptists before them, the early Quakers were seekers, earnest searchers for religious truth who found it helpful to meet regularly for prayers and Bible study.[7] In England, for over one hundred years, there had existed groups of seekers who prayed for God to move by his Spirit and power. They were not to be disappointed, as George Fox would soon take up his apostolic mantle and forge a heritage for future generations. David Edwards has described this period, 'the 1640s and 1650s saw also a ferment of sects voicing religious and social aspirations of those previously dispossessed: the Diggers, the Levellers, the Ranters, the Quakers and others'.[8] It was an age of religious turbulence.[9]

A perusal of the ministry of the early founder/leader of early Quakerism in Britain, George Fox, reveals that there were prophetic and miraculous elements. On numerous occasions he prayed for those with spiritual, physical, or mental health needs; he also witnessed miracles of healing, as a result of his prayers. Fox's preaching was inspirational, being Christ-centred, and Word-centred; he proclaimed a word of faith, life, and power; he convicted his hearers, even though many of them were not particularly well-disposed towards him or to Quakerism. His preaching, which included a call to pacifism, was controversial. He preached many times outside of church buildings, after the conclusion of public services of worship. Amid great antagonism from the people, and from ordained

---

[4] M.E. Hirst, *The Quakers in Peace and War: An Account of their Peace Principles and Practice* (London: Swarthmore Press, 1923), p. 115.

[5] Hirst, *The Quakers in Peace and War*, p. 132.

[6] G. Guiton, 'Seventeenth Century Quaker Pacifism', *Reviews in Religion and Theology* 9 (Sept. 2002), p. 294.

[7] Durnbaugh, *The Believers' Church*, p. 109.

[8] D.L. Edwards, *Christianity The First Two Thousand Years* (London: Cassell, 1997) p. 384.

[9] Gardner and Wenborn, *The History Today Companion to British History*, p. 318.

ministers, Fox preached in order that his listeners would become possessors of Christ's light and salvation. So radical and controversial was Fox's preaching, that he was forced to spend more than six years of his life incarcerated in various prisons across England, because of it. Fox could not have envisaged that he would fall victim to such brutal treatment whilst in pursuit of his calling.

It was in 1646, at the age of 22 years, when Fox experienced, what he called, the 'inner light'. He realised the experience of conversion, and he declared that 'the Father of Life, drew me to his Son, by his Spirit, and Grace'. Many of Fox's insights and preaching themes stemmed from the lengthy times he spent in prayer and solitude. These experiences proved to be a resource for the renewal of his inner strength and his ongoing communion with God. Fox believed in, and practised the leading of God's Spirit in his ministry, and frequently used the terms, in his *Journal*, 'I was moved upon', or 'I was moved of the Lord', implying that he felt an inner prompting to take him on a particular course of action.

Fox believed that he preached the message of the Gospel in continuity with the Early Church Apostles and pursued this with great enthusiasm throughout his life; testimonies from both his followers and his opponents attest to this. As an evangelist, Fox was deeply committed to the centrality of the Bible, to its power through the work of God's Spirit in his hearers, and to it as a source of final authority in matters of life, and church doctrine.

Fox was an evangelist by lifestyle. Donald Durnbaugh has depicted George Fox 'as a charismatic leader, who roamed around the British Isles, driven by his inward callings'.[10]

Fox was a special messenger and leader in a new movement of God. In the early years, his message was communicated predominantly through preaching rather than by written tract. He preached with intense conviction, a prophetic message of 'primitive Christianity revived' because, in his assessment, the professional Christianity of his day appeared to him unreal.[11]

A man named Brown, on his deathbed, prophesied that Fox would undertake a life of service and would be enabled by the Lord. Following Brown's funeral, Fox, for a period of about fourteen

---

[10] Durnbaugh, *The Believers Church*, p. 141.
[11] Durnbaugh, *The Believers Church*, p. 54.

days, went through a process of heart-softening, during which God's Spirit prepared him for the ministry, in fulfilment of Brown's prophecy.[12] Not only was Fox's work for God prophesied, but prophecy itself became an integral part of his own ministry. He reported, 'the Lord's power broke forth; and I had great openings and prophecies and spoke unto them [the people] of the things of God'.[13]

The role of prophecy and discernment within Gorge Fox's ministry were far-reaching in their purpose and application.[14] They helped him to 'read' difficult situations. He had the ability to sift through hostile crowds, often intent upon bringing him harm or violence, delivering his message with a timeliness and relevance due to his spiritual insights. He displayed an obvious compassion for those who were in need, and he frequently brought a relevant word or insight into the lives of those with whom he met, as he was moved upon to do so.[15]

Noble includes insights into the ministry of Fox. 'He fasted, prayed, argued ... he clarified his beliefs, guided – he was convinced – by direct communication with God, without the help of any man, book or writing'. Further, 'this young man spoke with the authority and in the language of an Old Testament prophet, denouncing professional ministers who failed to practise what they preached'.[16]

With 'superabundant energy', Fox brought a message of vitality and contentment for the soul at a time when the social and religious life of England was in turmoil.[17] He often verbally overpowered those with whom he clashed, claiming direct communication with God, for himself, and for everybody who would accept his message.[18] Fox believed that he was called of God for the times in which he lived. Fox's own commission came to him prophetically as he walked in the fields. At this time God instructed him to preach Jesus Christ's everlasting gospel and kingdom, of the inward light, Spirit,

---

12 V. Noble, *The Man in Leather Breeches* (London: Elek, 1953), p. 18.
13 *George Fox's Journal*, p. 19.
14 *George Fox's Journal*, p. 64.
15 *George Fox's Journal*, p. 67.
16 Noble, *The Man in Leather Breeches*, p. 41.
17 Noble, *The Man in Leather Breeches*, p. 45.
18 Noble, *The Man in Leather Breeches*, p. 45.

and grace.[19] Fox claimed that as he came increasingly influenced by the Spirit of God, wonderful depths and insights were opened up to him, beyond description.[20]

Crucial for Quakerism, was the prophecy which came to Fox, when he stood upon Pendle Hill, Lancashire, facing toward Cumbria, where 'the Lord let me see in what places he had a great people to be gathered'.[21] This prophecy was later fulfilled when Swarthmore Hall – the home of Judge and Margaret Fell, at Ulverston – in Cumbria, became the headquarters of the Quaker movement. Fox later married Margaret Fell, following the death of her husband.

The nature of George Fox's ministry – dynamic, public, and controversial – like all such ministry has to be able to withstand the rigours of scrutiny and criticism. Several questions emerge: how genuine were Fox's prophecies? Were his prophecies fulfilled? Or, were they simply inventions for his *Journal*? Such questions might be answered by consideration of the early stirrings of God's Spirit upon Fox's young life. He had a special inclination in his heart and life towards prayer and righteousness. The work of God's Spirit was evident in his preaching, and in his prayers for the sick. A man who suffered for his personal faith, preaching and inner convictions, would be unlikely to embellish his own stories, which would bring upon himself even more suffering and humiliation. The credibility of Fox's prophecies is observed in their fulfilment. Fox's record of Brown's prophecy relating to his own ministry, and Fox's prophecy on Pendle Hill – in which he depicted the birth and growth of Quakerism, initially in the North-West of England, and later, well beyond – were fulfilled.

The period of the birth of Quakerism, was significant in testing Fox's pastoral and leadership gifts. It was essential that when he visited and revisited the fast-emerging, scattered Quaker communities, he was able to encourage, motivate, discipline, and teach them as appropriate for their immediate situation. These persecuted groups of believers often needed uplifting in their spirits and strengthening in their minds. In this task, Fox excelled. William Penn – attesting

---

[19] Noble, *The Man in Leather Breeches*, p. 45.
[20] Noble, *The Man in Leather Breeches*, p. 45.
[21] C.W. Sharman, *George Fox and the Quakers* (London: QHS, 1991), pp. 78-82.

to this aspect of Fox's ministry – wrote that George Fox's ministry was powerful in that he possessed 'an extraordinary gift in opening the Scriptures; he would get to the marrow of things'.[22]

George Fox's *Book of Miracles* records over one hundred and seventy-five references to miracles or healing events during his ministry.[23] He and others visited the sick 'in the Lord's power and word … and by the same power to heal and strengthen'.[24] Fox encouraged the use of medicines mingled with faith in his pursuit of healing for the sick. In one example, he was moved upon to pray for one John Cartwright, who was ill with a fever, and as he prayed Fox 'felt an intercession for his life'.[25] The work of the God's Spirit upon Fox was in evidence, both in his preaching, and in his prayers for deliverance of the sick. Fox, in another example, when visiting Mansfield Woodhouse, ministered to a 'distracted' (probably mentally or emotionally disturbed) woman, who had been brought before him bound, in order to restrain her. Upon seeing her plight, Fox ministered peace and tranquillity to her. He recorded of this incident, 'the Lord's power settled her mind, and she mended; and afterwards she received the truth and continued in it to her death'.[26] This example serves to show the compassion Fox felt towards those who were sick.

Whilst the miraculous is evident in Fox's ministry, there was much scepticism around at the time, particularly from those of cessationist persuasion – they claimed that spiritual gifts had ceased after the New Testament period. Quakers were accused of 'pretend miracles', of being publishers of false lies, miracles, visions, prophecies, and doctrines.[27] Not all prayers for the sick were immediately answered, and reports of Fox's intentions to pray for the sick were often received with criticism.

Fox's pastoral empathy and motivations were clearly demonstrated when he met with Oliver Cromwell in order to persuade him to stem the tide of persecution arrayed against the Quakers. Fox

---

[22] William Penn, in *George Fox's Journal*, p. xxii.

[23] P. Anderson, in H.J. Cadbury, *George Fox's 'Book of Miracles'* (Philadelphia: QUIP, 2000), p. xvix.

[24] P. Anderson, in *George Fox's 'Book of Miracles'*, p. 161.

[25] J. Hull in *George Fox's 'Book of Miracles'*, p. 53.

[26] *George Fox's Journal*, pp. 88-89.

[27] *George Fox's Journal*, p. 17.

must have made an impact upon Cromwell, for Noble depicts Cromwell's warmth and emotion at their first meeting, later bidding Fox farewell, and requesting that they meet again.[28] In this and many other incidents, Fox's sense of God's leading, and his discernment, were acute.

The role of prophecy and other charismatic gifts in early Quakerism were apparent, primarily for the purpose of elevating Jesus Christ, in Spirit-empowered evangelistic ministry, which was instrumental in bringing many into faith, spiritual life, assurance, and healing.

Anderson's tribute to George Fox is fitting:

> He was a radical prophetic voice speaking out against societal ills and injustice … a charismatic challenger of institutionalised religion … a visionary who had special access to divine leadings … with a ministry growing out of a transforming encounter with the Power and Presence of God.[29]

Fox assumed the role of pastor and teacher, and leader, of a growing body of believers spread across England and beyond. As his ministry developed, his influence spread geographically, and with it the growth of Quakerism. The early Quakers were well organised, and their preachers (men and women) supplied the pulpits of non-Quaker churches upon request.[30] Fox's charismatic gifting was fully utilized in building up, encouraging, and enhancing the faith of Quakers.

In summary, Fox's ministry might be described as: radical, controversial, Spirit-empowered and led; prophetic, and miraculous in its scope. Fox was called and commissioned for his life-long work in a period of religious and political tensions, scepticism, violence, and persecution, in seventeenth-century England. He sought to bring an effective word of life and power to his hearers, and this was at great personal cost, in suffering more than six years incarcerated in various prisons.

Fox was a pastor, and leader of a scattered, persecuted group of believers, the Quakers – the Society of Friends. Their core beliefs

---

[28] Noble, *The Man in Leather Breeches*, p. 90.

[29] P. Anderson, in *George Fox's 'Book of Miracles'*, p. xxv.

[30] Robert Barclay, *The Inner Life of the Religious Societies of the Commonwealth* (London: H&S, c. 1876), p. 268

and intentions were to have the mind and disposition of Jesus
Christ in their day and time. This led them to live out lives of compassion, non-violence, and pacifism, in a hostile and increasingly
militaristic world.

Whilst the influences upon early Pentecostalism have been attributed to Methodism, and to the Holiness movement, there are
also many parallels with George Fox, and the early Quaker movement:

It is appropriate to note that George Fox attempted to embrace
the faith and practice of Christianity as depicted by the Early
Church and its apostolic ministry as described in the Book of Acts.
In so doing, Fox embraced its pacifist, non-violent message. Fox's
enduring legacy is in that he provides a relevant model of prophetic,
Spirit-empowered and enabled ministry for the contemporary
Church of Jesus Christ worldwide. In the ministry of George Fox,
a leader of stature within the formative years of Quakerism in Britain, there are a number of distinctive parallels to early Pentecostalism in Britain.

Although Pentecostalism developed in Britain some two-hun-
dred and fifty years or so after the time of George Fox, early Pentecostalism also embraced inspirational, Christ-centred, and Word-
centred preaching, and this was expected by those who attended its
public services of worship. Prophetic elements often formed a part
of the preaching,[31] and in the public/corporate worship, believers
practised spiritual gifts. Prayers for the sick were frequently offered,
with the laying on of hands by the church pastors and leaders. Miracles were anticipated as believers were encouraged to have faith on
behalf of those who were sick. George Fox modelled his ministry
upon that of the Early Church – thus he embraced the prophetic,
healing, and pacifism, as a part of the Church's legacy. Fox accepted
God's ability to heal the sick; he objected to war and militarism as
they were incompatible to the mind of Christ – he embraced pacifism and non-violence, its faith and worldview. Whilst pacifism
within early Pentecostalism was to some extent suppressed under
Boddy's leadership during the first early period of the movement in

---

[31] Particularly with reference to End Time events.

Britain, arguably, it came more to prominence, among the second-generation leaders of the movement.[32]

It is clear from these reflections on George Fox's life and ministry exactly why the mind of Christ, healing, and pacifism were for Booth-Clibborn 'non-negotiable', and integral to his evangelical faith, and teaching.

---

[32] Notably: Donald Gee, John Carter, Howard Carter, and numerous others.

8

THE LEGACIES OF A.A. BODDY AND A.S. BOOTH-CLIBBORN

Alfred Alexander Boddy died on the 10th September 1930. A local obituary[1] in memory of Boddy is presented below in full, and reads:

A.A. Boddy
Former Vicar of All Saints
Work on Wearside Recalled

The death occurred yesterday at Prior's Hallgarth, Pittington, of the Rev, Alexander Alfred Boddy, Vicar of Hallgarth Church, Pittington, and formerly of All Saints, Monkwearmouth. Mr Boddy had not enjoyed good health for a considerable time, especially since the death of his wife two years ago but had only been confined to the house for a few days. His death at the age of 75 will be mourned by a wide circle of friends on Wearside, for his 38 years' ministry in Monkwearmouth won him the esteem of everyone in the town. The son of the rector of Elwick (Co Durham), Mr Boddy used to say that he had a good deal of Methodist blood in his veins, for he was a descendant of Mrs Vazeille, a Hugenot, who married John Wesley, the pioneer of Methodism.

---

[1] In the: *Sunderland Echo and Shipping Gazzette* (11 Sept 1930), p. 5, courtesy of Sunderland City Libraries (accessed 5.12.2016).

INTENDED FOR LAW

Educated at Manchester Grammar School and University College, Durham, he was intended for the law and was articled to Messrs Worsley and Parker, solicitors, of Manchester. He was admitted as a solicitor of the Supreme Court of Judicature in 1876, by Sir George Jessel, Master of the Rolls, and practised in Manchester for some time.

Subsequently he was ordained deacon in 1880 and priest in 1881 by Bishop Lightfoot. He first held the curacy of Elwick Hall and Sedgefield, later ministering at St. Helen's, Low Fell, and at St. Peter's, Bishop Auckland, before going to All Saint's, Monkwearmouth, in 1884, as curate-in-charge. Two years later he was appointed vicar. The parish was a large one at that time, with a population of about 7,000. It has an even bigger population now, but the area has been reduced by about one-half.

AUTHOR OF TRAVEL BOOKS

His ministry in Monkwearmouth, which he frequently referred to as 'thirty-eight years beside a steam-hammer' – a reference to the proximity of the church and vicarage to the ironworks – was a most successful one. During his 38 years there he preached more than 3,000 times, married 835 couples, baptized 2,770 children and prepared more than 600 for confirmation. During the early years of his ministry, Mr Boddy travelled widely and in 1885 he was made a Fellow of the Royal Geographical Society. A number of his travel books, such as 'To Kairwan, the Holy', 'Scenes in Mohammedan Africa', 'With Russian Pilgrims at the White Sea Monastery', 'By Ocean, Prairie and Peak', 'Journeys in British Columbia', 'Christ in his Holy Land', and 'Days in Galilee', enjoyed a wide sale and considerable reputation when published. In 1890, Mr Boddy married Miss Pollock, the daughter of a Yorkshire clergyman. As Vicar of Monkwearmouth, he played a prominent part in organizing relief measures for the families of the miners and ironworkers during the Durham Miner's strike of 1892.

'SPEAKING WITH TONGUES'

The Pentecostal Movement, which found a Sunderland home at All Saint's Church, created something of a sensation in the town at the time. At the meetings conducted by Mr Boddy from 1907 till the outbreak of the War in 1914, there were some remarkable manifestations. It was claimed that angels were to be seen in the church, while numerous cases of 'speaking with tongues' were reported. Visitors from all over Britain, Australia, America, Germany, Holland, Syria, and even China were drawn to the meetings, which were of the revival type.[2] The inscription of the foundation stone of All Saint's Parish Hall, Fulwell, which reads: 'When the fire of the Lord fell it burned up the debt', is a relic of this period in the church history.

In 1922 Mr Boddy accepted the living of Pittington Hallgarth, near Durham, where he has worked for eight years and made many friends. He leaves one son, Mr James A. Boddy, of Thurcaston (Leicestershire), and two daughters, one of whom is Mrs Reginald Taylor, the wife of a missionary in Western China. The funeral will take place at Pittington on Saturday.

From the above, it is apparent that Boddy was a popular clergyman, who had enjoyed wide esteem. He had travelled extensively and had been a writer of published travel-books of considerable reputation; a Fellow of the Royal Geographical Society, and a well-known Church leader among the many families of miners and iron-workers in and around Sunderland. This article clearly endorses Boddy's association with early Pentecostalism, locally and internationally. The 'meetings' referred to is a reference to Boddy's Sunderland Conventions. The obituary demonstrates that Boddy had a great love for his pastoral work, and this led him into the homes and lives of his many parishioners, where he was widely respected.

Whilst Boddy was a caring pastor who sought to lead his flock into relevant biblical teaching: that God is love, which extends directly to humankind; that the Holy Spirit brings love and unity among believers, and so on; in many areas, the teaching of Boddy was biblically based, and prescriptive. On his position as a patriot,

---

[2] Bold typeface in the original.

and defender of militarism, his views were not well-argued. Pacifists might justifiably assert that it is impossible to hold to the biblical truths of Christian love and unity that Boddy espoused in the pages of *Confidence*, as significant and important, but then to abandon them in time of war. Over and above Boddy's clearly stated teaching, hovers the cloud of militarism and war, which he supported. In this he was an activist, and this is demonstrated by the way in which he edited and directed *Confidence* – a strongly influential voice within early Pentecostalism in Britain and beyond – through the war years and in the years that followed. As this book has pointed out, Boddy was a life-long patriot, and he saw no problem with the use of militarism as a means of solving international disputes, this is beyond doubt. But, in his extensive writing he made little attempt to justify his position from a biblical standpoint. He did, however, in the pages of *Confidence* suppress the publication of articles that were of the pacifist view, and where he chose to allow such references, he invariably published articles endorsing patriotism or militarism, in the pages immediately following such articles, in the same issue.

Readers of *Confidence* might well have drawn a conclusion that patriotism was the only position held and endorsed within early Pentecostalism in Britain. This is misleading, for the seeds of pacifism were already taking root at the time of Boddy, not least due to the influence of Booth-Clibborn and others, within Pentecostalism in Britain, and this became more apparent among the next (or second) generation of leaders as they emerged. The views of Boddy were also at odds with a leading Pentecostal group in the USA, the Assemblies of God, as they had seriously reviewed, endorsed, and accepted the views of Booth-Clibborn, as expressed in *Blood Against Blood*, and had written pacifism into their Constitution, in the years 1914-1917.[3]

Richard Massey has provided insights into how pacifism was differently received by listeners in Pentecostal meetings at two different locations. He outlined the situation:

A valuable insight into the British scene at the beginning of the war is given by Frank Bartleman [the American pacifist, preacher] when he returned through London from the

---

[3] See notes in Chapter 5.

Continent on his way to America in 1914. He reveals the emerging conflict of attitudes towards pacifism: 'I spoke once at the
Central Pentecostal Mission. The Lord gave me a strong message against the war spirit in Christians. The leader said that if
he were a young man, he would enlist himself. They were opening their meetings with a "War Hymn" … my message dropped
like a bomb [sic] in the camp'. Bartleman by contrast spoke
shortly afterwards at Pastor A.E. Saxby's assembly: 'Here God
gave me a strong message against the war spirit also. But it was
very differently received. The leader thanked me warmly.'[4]

Massey, citing Robinson, continued:

These two accounts reveal the two contrasting attitudes within
Pentecostalism. Polhill and Boddy with their links to the Church
of England increasingly became more patriotic in their stance.
Whereas Saxby, who seems to have been greatly influenced by
the strongly pacifist views of William Booth's son-in-law, Arthur
Booth-Clibborn, gathered around him a number of active pacifists, some of whom were to become conscientious objectors.[5]

Massey's accounts provide a clear insight into the beginnings of
the division that would develop as the war-years (1914-1918) progressed, and beyond. The second generation of leaders, which included Gee – encouraged by his pastor, Saxby, (described by Gee as
'a strong pacifist'), who had been influenced by Booth-Clibborn –
along with a number of others, suffered for their pacifist faith, and
were likely to distance themselves from those who may have espoused militarism.

Boddy clearly demonstrated numerous pastoral and leadership
qualities, which have, in recent times, been recognised and valued.
He also made a huge contribution to early Pentecostalism in Britain.
However, his overt patriotism, whilst repeatedly asserted from the
outbreak of WWI, was unconvincingly argued in the pages of *Confidence*, this was from its beginning under Boddy's exclusive editorial
control. This created a confusing, if not misleading, legacy for Pentecostalism in Britain, and beyond. Whilst Boddy has, in recent

---

[4] Richard D. Massey, 'Sound and Scriptural Union' (PhD thesis, Birmingham
University, 1987), pp. 250-51.
[5] Massey, 'Sound and Scriptural Union', p. 251.

times, been appropriately commended for his ecumenical endeavours – he worked consistently to develop friendships and positive relationships with ministers from other churches, including Anglican, Congregationalist, and Methodist churches – he failed to unify the growing patriotic versus pacifist divide within the Pentecostal movement, and by the absence of column inches in *Confidence*, he chose not to recognise or to validate pacifist faith. It is a sad reflection that his influential ministry was to some extent undermined by the confusion that he generated through the pages of *Confidence* and that exacerbated the patriotic-pacifist divide within early Pentecostalism in Britain, thereby sowing seeds of confusion over this issue for later generations of Pentecostals.[6]

Allan Anderson has summarised Boddy's situation at this time:

> Early British Pentecostal denominations were essentially pacifist organizations and the issue effectively ended their relationship with the patriotic Anglicans. Boddy regularly publishing patriotic statements, news and letters from British soldiers in *Confidence* must have alienated many British Pentecostals who believed strongly that they should abstain from any involvement in this end-time conflagration. In any event, the Great War effectively ended the leadership of Boddy and Polhill over the British Pentecostal movement and its missionaries.[7]

Anderson here partly attributes Boddy's patriotism to his loss of leadership within early Pentecostalism in Britain. Further, he has observed:

> Among other reasons, the fundamental difference between the pacifist and non-pacifist views within British Pentecostalism was ultimately to lead to the separation of Boddy and Polhill from the movement in the 1920s and the setting up of the Assemblies of God.[8]

Cornelis van der Laan, has contributed a number of insights into early Pentecostalism prior to, and during the Great War: Bartleman, an American, preacher, writer, and pacifist, had 'warned against the

---

[6] Including among my own family members.
[7] Anderson, *Spreading Fires*, p. 228.
[8] Anderson, *Spreading Fires*, p. 228.

war spirit he experienced among Christians in Germany and England'. Further, that 'the war placed a heavy burden on the unity of
the Spirit among European Pentecostals'.[9] On Boddy's leadership
of early Pentecostalism, he wrote further:

> Boddy's stand in the war combined with his refusal to cooperate
> on the after-war developments to organise British Pentecostal-
> ism as an independent force, resulted in his loss of leadership'.[10]

On the position of the Dutch pastor, Gerit Roelof Polman, who
had worked alongside Booth-Clibborn in the Salvation Army, Cornelis van der Laan further commented:

> Somewhere between November 1907 and March 1908 a corre-
> spondence between Boddy and Polman began, that developed
> into a warm relationship.[11]

Polman, however, adopted a strong pacifist position – countering
Boddy's position, and that of *Confidence* – stating that war 'is anti-
Christian',[12] and that 'nationalism was threatening the unity of the
children of God of different nationalities'.[13] It is understandable
that 'the contacts between Boddy and Polman also declined',[14] after
a few years, following the war. A similar decline in the relationship
between Boddy and Booth-Clibborn occurred, following the early
Sunderland Conventions.

Arthur Sydney Booth-Clibborn has been acknowledged as a capable leader and evangelist, within the Salvation Army in Europe,
and as a respected patriarchal figure, within early Pentecostalism in
Britain. Whilst James Robinson has suggested that he had only 'one
theme', that of anti-militarism, this fails to recognise the importance of the bigger picture: Booth-Clibborn tried to live out the
Quaker principles that he adopted in his youth; to have the mind of
Christ, and to apply pacifist teaching of non-violence, and peace-

---

[9] Cornelis van der Laan, 'Alexander Boddy: Anglican Father of Dutch Pentecostalism', *Journal of the European Pentecostal Theological Association* 31.1. (2011), p.
106, citing Frank Bartleman, *Two Years Mission Work In Europe* (Los Angeles, by
author, undated), p. 37.

[10] van der Laan, 'Alexander Boddy', p. 107.

[11] van der Laan, 'Alexander Boddy', p. 96.

[12] van der Laan, 'Alexander Boddy', p. 107.

[13] van der Laan, 'Alexander Boddy', p. 107.

[14] van der Laan, 'Alexander Boddy', p. 109.

making, throughout his life and extensive ministry. For him, war and militarism were incompatible with the Christian faith, and the overt teaching of Jesus was non-negotiable.

Booth-Clibborn articulated Christian pacifism in his book, *Blood Against Blood*, and this work was influential within Pentecostalism in Britain and in America. In it, he argued for Christian pacifism: based upon Jesus' teaching, grounded in biblical principles, with an appeal to the history of the Early Church, the Church Fathers, and to Christian and Social History. Booth-Clibborn argued his case so thoroughly, systematically and convincingly, that the book was banned in Britain when military conscription was introduced during WWI in 1916.

Booth-Clibborn was able to influence numerous young believers, some of whom would become the second generation of leaders within Pentecostalism in Britain. It is apparent that his influence was not in any way limited by denomination or geography. His primitive Quaker faith, linked with radical Christianity, and pacifism – integral to both – was part and parcel of who he was.
Donald Gee reflected:

> A.S. Booth-Clibborn, who came from old Quaker stock, presented his own view in no half-hearted manner, and probably helped to influence many. The Military Service Act legally provided for consideration of conscientious objection, and a number of young men connected with the Pentecostal Movement went before the tribunals. They mostly passed through hard experiences, particularly at the beginning ... God blessed to their souls what was often sheer persecution.[15]

Arthur Sydney Booth-Clibborn died on 12 February 1939. In Redemption Tidings,[16] an obituary in his memory was written by John Carter:

> A Great Warrior is Called to Rest.
> Death of A.S. Booth-Clibborn.
> A well-known character in Pentecostal circles for the past quarter of a century has been called home. Our aged brother, Arthur

---

[15] Donald Gee, *Wind and Flame* (Croydon: Heath Press, 1967), p. 102.
[16] John Carter, *Redemption Tidings* 15.6 (March 10, 1939), p. 7.

Sydney Booth-Clibborn, after a long warfare for the kingdom of God, is now at rest from his labours. He was a frequent visitor at the Pentecostal Conventions in Kingsway Hall, and on the occasion of the visit to London of his well-known son (William Booth-Clibborn) a few years ago, it was a great pleasure to see the father, the mother (the Marechale), and son on the Kingsway platform together, during one of our Conventions. During the Great War, A.S. Booth-Clibborn was a great friend and supporter of Pentecostal 'conscientious objectors' and spoke on their behalf at many tribunals, whilst his book 'Blood against Blood' assisted many in the right attitude a Christian should take to war.

The following paragraph is taken from 'The Christian Herald':-

In the passing of the late Commissioner A.S. Booth-Clibborn, husband of 'The Marechale', a valiant soldier of the Cross has been lost to us. Mr.Booth-Clibborn came of a distinguished Quaker ancestry. He was converted in 1875 through a wave from the Moody revival while he was in business in Northern Ireland and soon became a recognised minister among the Society of Friends. On the invitation of General Booth, he entered the Salvation Army and took up work on the Continent, for which he was specially suited, as he spoke four languages fluently. In Switzerland he pioneered the work in association with Miss Catherine Booth, who later became his wife, witnessing remarkable blessing, although meeting with fierce opposition. They were twice imprisoned, endured much physical suffering, their halls sacked and their lives threatened, but they were miraculously saved. They persisted, however, in their campaigns, and hundreds were converted. Mr. Booth-Clibborn was a born poet and he composed no less than three hundred hymns, many in French and Dutch, as well as in German and English. The prayers and sympathy of our readers will go out to the Marechale and family in their great loss.

This tribute recalls a number of aspects in the life and ministry of Booth-Clibborn: that he was known and acknowledged within the early years of Pentecostalism in Britain; he was a visitor to the movement's annual conventions; by his strong pacifist stand, he was able to influence many young believers, and he was a supporter of Pentecostals who were conscientious objectors, and defended them and others at their tribunals. The importance of Booth-Clibborn's book, *Blood Against Blood*, and its influence, is noted by John Carter, the obituary writer, together with the choice of words: that his book had 'assisted many in the right attitude a Christian should take to war', this provided a fitting legacy to Booth-Clibborn's life-long work and ministry. He was able to link the overt teaching of Jesus, the events of his Crucifixion and Death, with the Early Church's distinctive pacifism – in the face of the displeasure of successive Roman Emperors, up to the time of Constantine. He then linked this with the witness of the Church Fathers; he espoused the exemplary pacifism of George Fox and the early Quakers. Booth-Clibborn's non-negotiable pacifism was Jesus-centred, Word-centred, and Spirit-centred, and for him, it was a clear expression of the mind of Christ for all Christians to portray in a world of unending militarism and war.

The editor of *Redemption Tidings* at the time of Booth-Clibborn's death was John Carter. In January of the same year, 1939, he wrote a lengthy article,[17] 'The Christian's Attitude to War'. This served to reiterate much of Booth-Clibborn's pacifist teaching for a new generation of readers. In his article, Carter referred to the religious leaders at the time of WWI, and their legacy of confusion, with some leaders maintaining that it was the duty of all young men to enlist in the fighting ranks, whilst others contended that war is anti-Christian and that it was therefore wrong and that it was therefore wrong for Christians to engage in warfare. Carter goes on to affirm that this issue should not be left to the conscience of the individual, as this is not an infallible guide to personal conduct, for as the Apostle Paul taught, the conscience may be at times unreliable.

---

[17] John Carter, *Redemption Tidings* 15.3 (Jan 27, 1939), pp. 1-3.

9

THE CONTEMPORARY SIGNIFICANCE OF PATRIOTISM AND PACIFISM

In this chapter, patriotism and pacifism are viewed from the perspective of the last one hundred years or so of history. Statistics are considered, which demonstrate the scale of devastation that ensued in two world wars, together with the current statistics for expenditure on armaments across the world. The views of scholars and writers who have lived during this period also are assessed, and an attempt is also made to assess the significance of these issues for the Church today.

Peter Brock and Nigel Young have suggested, that 'at the outset of the twentieth century the prospects for continuing world peace looked promising',[1] but this was soon to change, for as they further observed:

> Few persons could have envisaged that within the first half of the twentieth century the world would be rocked by two successive wars of catastrophic dimensions.[2]

---

[1] Peter Brock and Nigel Young, *Pacifism in the Twentieth Century* (Toronto: University of Toronto Press, 1999), p. 3.
[2] Brock and Young, *Pacifism*, p. 3.

The statistics of World War I (hereafter WWI), in summary reveal: WWI cost 30 million lives and £80,000m.[3] In contrast, there
were those opposed to militarism in all its forms: in WWI there
were 16,000 (est.) conscientious objectors; 0.125% of the 6 million
enlisted. Niall Ferguson has proposed that WWI was the 'greatest
error of modern history',[4] a verdict endorsed by many pacifists, and
others, who resisted the war. Rachel Barker established that 'three
out of every ten objectors in WWI spent some time in civil or military prisons'.[5] Marwick records that there were 1,500 'intractable
absolutists', whose challenge to the authority of the state, the government simply could not comprehend; about 70 men died from
their prison treatment'.[6] During WWI, the treatment of pacifists
taking a stand as conscientious objectors was often little short of
barbaric at the hands of the military authorities.

Niall Ferguson asked a number of searching questions in his
analysis of WWI and its outcomes, such as: Was the war inevitable?
Why did Britain's leaders decide to intervene when war broke out
on the continent of Europe? Was the war, as is often asserted, really
greeted with popular enthusiasm? Did propaganda keep the war going? Who won the peace – or to be precise, who ended up paying
for the war?[7] These are questions that few, at the time, or since, have
asked. Ferguson, writing from a factual, historical perspective also
writes of the myths of militarism.[8]

The statistics relating to World War II (1939–1945), (hereafter
WWII), also paint a grim picture of its outcomes:

> 21 million young men were killed in battle, 15-20 million women,
> children and old people killed in air raids, 29.5 million wounded,
> mutilated or incapacitated for work, 21.25 million lost their
> homes through air raids, 45 million evacuated, deported or

---

[3] Unknown author, *I Am Persuaded* (New Malden: Fellowship Of Reconciliation, 1956, 1958, 1970), p. 7, citing figures quoted in International Review of
Diplomatic and Political Science.

[4] Niall Ferguson, *The Pity of War* (London: Penguin, 1998), p. 462.

[5] Rachel Barker, *Conscience, Government and War*, p. 119, citing Dennis Hayes,
Challenge of Conscience, 1949.

[6] Arthur Marwick, *A History of the Modern British Isles, 1914–1999: Circumstances, Events and Outcomes* (Oxford: Blacknell, 2000), p. 50.

[7] Ferguson, *The Pity of War*, p. xxv.

[8] Ferguson, *The Pity of War*, p. 1.

interned, 30 million homes reduced to ashes, 150 million people left without shelter, prey to famine and disease.[9]

In WWII, there were 59,000 (est.) conscientious objectors, 1.2% of the 5 million called up to serve in the armed forces.[10] Whilst their treatment frequently resulted in prison sentences, arguably, the plight of conscientious objectors in WWII marginally improved over and above the situation of WWI. Rachel Barker examined the plight of many conscientious objectors, and their treatment by the government and military authorities, during WWII. Barker provided statistics from the numerous tribunals that were held around the country, as a result of the applications for exemption from military service. The statistics cover the period, 1939-1944, (the figures for 1945 being unavailable): 3,072 conscientious objectors were registered unconditionally before the tribunals (Category A registration). 29,176 were registered conditionally, subject to undertaking civilian work or training (Category B registration). 21,900 were registered, but liable to be called up for non-combatant duties (Category C registration), and approximately 23,000 had their names removed from the register because of the applicants' failure to convince the tribunal (Category D registration).[11]

Following the ordeal of a rigorous tribunal, many conscientious objectors found themselves in the position of trying to find employment, a task that proved difficult if not impossible. Rachel Barker has provided statistics to underline the scale of this problem: fifty County, City, and Borough Councils, dismissed all conscientious objectors from their employment.[12] Twenty such councils took steps to dismiss conscientious objectors for the duration of WWII.[13] This included school teachers in some areas.[14] In 1940, the Ministry of Labour was made aware that 2,000 conscientious objectors, who had been told to obtain alternative work in agriculture and forestry, 'had found it impossible to obtain employment'.[15] Many pacifists in WWII, when they chose to register as

---

[9] Unknown Author, *I Am Persuaded*, p. 7.
[10] Barker, *Conscience, Government and War*, p. 121.
[11] Barker, *Conscience, Government and War*, p. 152.
[12] Barker, *Conscience, Government and War*, p. 69.
[13] Barker, *Conscience, Government and War*, p. 69.
[14] Barker, *Conscience, Government and War*, p. 72.
[15] Barker, *Conscience, Government and War*, p. 45.

conscientious objectors, not only had to face unsympathetic tribunals, but they were also frequently faced with the prospect of rejection by numerous employers, particularly those within local government.

Ferguson has included an insight into the new rules of engagement applicable in WWII:

> death for deserters … violence against civilians … no quarter for prisoners. This truly was 'total war' … calculated to make that war one of unprecedented violence, in which men on both sides fought to the end because they no longer had any alternative.[16]

Such was the stark escalation of the hardening of the rules of engagement used in warfare during WWII, over and above the trench warfare of WWI.

Not all pacifists were Christians. The social/political influences of pacifism are identified by Brock and Young, who observe, 'socialist antimilitarism, which emerged, along with the organised labour movement in the half century before 1914'.[17] The list of respected twentieth century pacifist activists is lengthy and is comprised of politicians of all persuasions, church leaders from across the denominations, community leaders, writers, and educators. Many pacifists owed a great debt to the few parliamentarians who defended their cause, and not least, their human rights, before successive governments. These were instrumental in changing the laws in order to secure fairer tribunals and balanced judgements for conscientious objectors. There were also a number of pacifist institutions, established by pacifists for the purpose of providing identity groups for a variety of pacifist persuasions. These groups, by means of membership and networking, newsletters, lobbying of parliament, and other initiatives, tried to help fellow pacifists in the cause. Such groups are considered in the next section.

Martin Ceadel, Professor of Politics at Oxford, has outlined some of the significant pacifist institutions: The No-Conscription Fellowship [N-CF] – a pacifist organisation comprised of many members of the early Independent Labour Party – was established

---

[16] Ferguson, *The Pity of War*, p. 394.
[17] Brock and Young, *Pacifism in the Twentieth Century*, p. 4.

in November 1914 by Fenner Brockway, with the specific aim to oppose conscription.[18] The No More War Movement, mainly pacifist, was established in 1921;[19] Fenner Brockway was the first editor of its journal, *No More War*, launched in February 1922;[20] the movement claimed to have a membership of 3,000 in 1927, but it wound up, merging with the Peace Pledge Union in 1937.[21] The Peace Pledge Union was established in May 1936, under the leadership of an Anglican clergyman, Dick Sheppard; its membership in April 1940 was 136,000.[22] The PPU, as it is now called, is still in existence today. The Fellowship of Reconciliation, founded in December 1914, with a membership (that included a large number of Anglican and Methodist ministers) of 3,300 in the late 1920's, rising to 9,813 in 1939. The FoR, as it is now known, is still in existence today.[23] The Methodist Peace Fellowship [MPF] is also in existence today and partners with FoR. War Resister's International [WRI], founded in 1921, at The Hague, moved to London in 1923. Today it represents the interests of conscientious objectors, and anti-war issues around the world.[24]

From Ceadel's statistics, it is seen that during WWI, some Anglican ministers were members of the Fellowship of Reconciliation; this suggested that not all Anglican ministers were in favour of the surge of patriotism and militarism that was being voiced widely within the state-church. Clive Barker has verified this situation regarding the Anglican Church's pacifist sympathisers in considerable detail.[25] The Methodist Peace Fellowship (MPF), founded by Rev. Henry Carter, boasted 5,000 members in 1940, 1,000 of whom were ministers.[26] Whilst only some of the pacifist institutions are considered above, the work of these groups has proved essential in communicating widely the pacifist arguments against war and

---

[18] Martin Ceadel, *Pacifism in Britain 1914–1945: The Defining of a Faith* (Oxford: Clarendon Press, 1980), p. 318.

[19] Ceadel, *Pacifism in Britain*, p. 318.

[20] Ceadel, *Pacifism in Britain*, p. 73.

[21] Ceadel, *Pacifism in Britain*, p. 318.

[22] Ceadel, *Pacifism in Britain*, p. 318.

[23] Ceadel, *Pacifism in Britain*, p. 317.

[24] Ceadel, *Pacifism in Britain*, p. 319.

[25] Clive Barker, *Subversive Peacemakers* (Cambridge: Lutterworth Press, 2014).

[26] Kenneth Greet, *P21C* (Methodist Peace Fellowship with Fellowship of Reconciliation), 32 (July 2009), p. 1, <www.mpf.org.uk> (accessed 1.6.2012).

militarism, by the regular publication of newsletters, and also in promoting wider participation, and by securing new membership. The work of pacifist institutions continues today, and has a wide role within politics and education, in voicing issues, such as arms control, nuclear disarmament, and peaceful coexistence around the world.

The numerous voices of Christian pacifism have influenced many, including those who might have preferred to refer to themselves as social or political pacifists. During the twentieth-century there have been a number of influential educators and writers of pacifist persuasion. Extracts from their contributions are included in the following pages.

The work of Arthur Sidney Booth-Clibborn, has been acknowledged as a primary source throughout this book, and as being influential within early Pentecostalism and beyond. In his book, *Blood Against Blood*, he initially protested against the Boer War (1889-1902). He wrote:

> The English and the Dutch are the races which first issued the Bible in the language of the people. On the eve of the twentieth century these two races are engaged in mortal conflict in South Africa.[27]

In this war, 5,744 British and 4,000 Dutch Boers were killed. Booth-Clibborn's view of war was that it is anti-Christian.[28] In his remarks, he unequivocally stated his Christian pacifist position as one of total opposition to war. He revised and re-published this work, just prior to WWI. It is not surprising that his strongly pacifist assertions led ultimately to the banning of the book by the British authorities in 1916, although it was at this time widely promoted by Christian pacifists within Pentecostalism in North America.

Leyton Richards, writing in the period between the two world wars, put forward the case for Christian pacifism. He recognised that war is constantly being prepared for among civilised peoples.[29] He argued that the process of war and the Gospel of Jesus can

---

[27] Booth-Clibborn, *Blood Against Blood*, p. 3.
[28] Booth-Clibborn, *Blood Against Blood*, pp. 5-6.
[29] Leyton Richards, *The Christian's Alternative to War* (London: Student Christian Movement Press, 1935), p. 24.

never be reconciled,[30] and that Christians 'are called to yield our obedience to his [God's] authority'.[31] He further argued that it is the nature of war that 'it not only kills the bodies of men, but it also degrades and destroys all that is finest in the soul'.[32] In his conclusion, Richards stated that 'if Christianity be qualified or jettisoned in favour of war, it is not a gospel of redemption but only second best'.[33]

Expanding on Richards' theme, G.H.C. Macgregor defended pacifism from the perspective of the New Testament. He argued that Jesus' example is essentially pacifist, and that in the Cross is 'an alternative method of meeting and overcoming evil which renders all violent methods obsolete'.[34] Macgregor further argued that war involves 'an utter prostitution of moral values ... the Christian conception of personal relationships [and] cannot under any conditions be brought within the orbit of the Christian ethic'.[35] Macgregor's defence of pacifism, in his book's later edition, addressed what he called, 'the latest defences of Christian non-pacifism'.[36]

Charles Raven's book,[37] based upon a series of lectures delivered at Boston University in 1950, provided a clear statement of the Christian pacifist case, in which Raven linked his own experience of the grace of Christ, the love of God, and the fellowship of the Spirit, to pacifist belief and practice.

Roland Bainton, writing during the time of the Cold War between east and west, provided a historical survey, that included an examination of the repeated failures of the world powers to eliminate war: he lamented, that following WWI – the war to end all wars – 'a four power treaty was signed in 1921 by the Unites States, Great Britain, France and Japan'. Its aim was to 'eliminate war by the

---

[30] Richards, *The Christian's Alternative to War*, p. 34.

[31] Richards, *The Christian's Alternative to War*, p. 48.

[32] Richards, *The Christian's Alternative to War*, p. 76.

[33] Richards, *The Christian's Alternative to War*, p. 97.

[34] G.H.C. Macgregor, *The New Testament Basis of Christian Pacifism* (London: FoR, 1953), p. 13.

[35] Macgregor, *The New Testament Basis*, p. 13.

[36] Macgregor, *The New Testament Basis*, preface.

[37] Charles Raven, *The Theological Basis of Christian Pacifism* (London: The Fellowship of Reconciliation, 1952).

reduction in armaments'.[38] Bainton recorded similar initiatives: the League of Nations, established in Paris in 1920; the Kellogg-Brand Pact, outlawing war, was signed in Paris by 65 states in 1928. All sought alternatives to the settlement of disputes among and between nations.[39] Bainton concluded, 'is there any possibility that the Christian word will be heard?'[40] He held a realistic view of the church-state situation, and suggested that it is not appropriate to 'invoke Christ to justify nuclear annihilation',[41] an obvious reference to the state-Church's practice of blessing warships and submarines, during launch ceremonies.

The writer, John D. Knox, a pacifist during WWII, argued that apostate [suggests abandoned principles] Christianity projects an image 'that worldly wars are the outworking of God's will and Christ's design in right against wrong, and as such demanding of a Christian's allegiance and that with worldly weapons'. Knox continued, 'this is a lie, a falsehood and a defamation of character – Christ's character'.[42]

Robert Clark, wrote as, 'one who accepts the Bible, rather than the church … as the final authority in the Christian life',[43] and did much to challenge the general readiness of Christians to participate in war. He wrote of the slippery slope that leads to war; he was convinced that people persuaded themselves to believe that wrong is right. Clark in summary asserted:

> Pacifism is not an impractical, woolly option for idealists who cannot face up to the world's realities, any more than Christianity is. In an age when mankind threatens to destroy itself it is the only rational course and the overwhelming consensus of biblical teaching and practice supports it.[44]

---

[38] Roland H. Bainton, *Christian Attitudes to War and Peace* (London: Hodder & Stoughton, 1961), p. 214.

[39] Bainton, *Christian Attitudes to War and Peace*, pp. 214-15.

[40] Bainton, *Christian Attitudes to War and Peace*, p. 264.

[41] Bainton, *Christian Attitudes to War and Peace*, p. 268.

[42] John D. Knox, *Eternal War, the Why? of Conscientious Objection* (Victoria, Australia: New Life Publications, 1967), p. 5.

[43] Robert Clark, *Does the Bible Teach Pacifism?* (London: Marshall's Paperbacks, 1983), p. 11.

[44] Clark, *Does the Bible Teach Pacifism?* Quotation, inside rear cover.

Originally written in earlier years, and then revised at the height of the Cold War, Clark's appeal to all Christians is that they should be under no illusions about the realities of war and must be men and women of peace.[45]

On this point, the research of Michel Desjardins is significant.[46] Following his detailed technical examination of the New Testament under the two headings of peace and violence, he concluded that whilst both are clearly evident:

> [the] core of the New Testament message promotes peace ... if you look at what Jesus himself really taught ... or even Paul – the real Paul – you will find that the focus lies on peace.[47]

This is a clear response for those who seek to justify war from selected New Testament passages.

Robert Clouse reminded his readers: 'we are taught not to steal from our neighbours, but that it is patriotic to defend the taking of territory in war'.[48]

On the contentious issue of disarmament, Kenneth Greet,[49] secretary to the Methodist Conference, chairperson of the World Methodist Council, member of FoR, and a life-long pacifist, proposed that the issue of peace and disarmament is 'the crucial moral issue of the age'.[50] Developing the theme further, Dana Mills-Powell brought together a number of leading evangelicals, in discussion.[51] Here, leaders stood for peace as an issue of faith. In summary, they objected, as with one voice, to the nuclear threat, and discussed the realities of world hunger, poverty, stewardship of the environment, and the need for spiritual revival.

Written at a point toward the end of the Cold War, Clive Barrett summarized the views of numerous contributors in their vision of

---

[45] Clark, *Does the Bible Teach Pacifism?*, p. 103.

[46] Michel Desjardins, *Peace, Violence and the New Testament* (Sheffield: Sheffield Academic Press, 1997).

[47] Desjardins, *Peace, Violence and the New Testament*, p. 118.

[48] Clouse (ed.), *War, Four Christian Views*, p. 196.

[49] Kenneth Greet, *The Big Sin* (London: Marshall Morgan & Scott, 1982).

[50] Greet, *The Big Sin*, p. 65.

[51] Dana Mills-Powell (ed.), *Decide for Peace* (Basingstoke: Marshall Morgan & Scott, 1986).

Christian pacifism.[52] They repudiated modern warfare, and re-
nounced war and all preparation to wage war. This book celebrated
the 50th anniversary of the foundation of the Anglican Pacifist Fellowship, and brought together a wide variety of backgrounds and
perspectives. Barrett summarized the issues, 'in a world threatened
by nuclear war, peace must be the goal we strive for'.[53] The contributors unanimously called for a radical acceptance in our hearts of
the gospel message of Jesus Christ.

The work of Christopher Catherwood has brought the discussion into the context of more recent times.[54] He wrote of themes
of mass murder, ethnic cleansing, and religious nationalism. The
issues of Islam and nationalism are also discussed,[55] as well as the
concept of the 'clash of civilisations'.[56] Catherwood has summarized:

> the new world order is replacing the bi-polar powers of the cold
> war and is characterised not only by the rise of new economic
> forces, a crumbling of old empires, and the discrediting of com-
> munism, but also by the resurgence of parochial identities based
> on ethnic and religious allegiances.[57]

These issues are relevant to the times in which we live, and rank
among the key issues facing humankind today.

In 2012, Norman Kember observed that there are not enough
young people involved with the Baptist Peace Fellowship.[58] This
must also be a concern among other pacifist organisations. There is
much to be done in terms of communicating the message of peace
among the younger generation.

A survey of 26 UK Universities in the period 2001–2006, revealed that 1,900 military projects were conducted, with a research

---

[52] Clive Barrett (ed.), *Peace Together, A Vision of Christian Pacifism* (Cambridge: James Clarke & Co., 1987).

[53] Barrett (ed.), *Peace Together,* Foreword.

[54] Christopher Catherwood, *Why the Nations Rage* (London: Hodder & Stoughton, 1997).

[55] Catherwood, *Why the Nations Rage,* p. 90.

[56] Catherwood, *Why the Nations Rage,* p. 95.

[57] Catherwood, *Why the Nations Rage,* p. 97, citing Mark Jurgensmeyer, *The New Cold War* (Oklahoma: University of Oklahoma Press, 1993), pp. 1-2.

[58] Norman Kember, *Baptist Peace Fellowship Newsletter* (Spring 2012), p. 2, www.bpf.org.uk (accessed 1.6.2012).

income to the group of a minimum of £725m.[59] A recent publication by the Fellowship of Reconciliation quoted the UK's armaments expenditure, as follows:

> The UK is now the fifth highest military spender in the world with an increased annual budget of £46 Bn announced in 2016.[60]

This is significant spending, but it is eclipsed by the United States, China, Saudi Arabia, and Russia, where military expenditure is £493Bn, £490Bn, £71.7Bn, and £54.6Bn, respectively.[61] With Global expenditure on armaments estimated at £1,378Bn.[62] From these figures it is seen that the issues of patriotism and rising nationalism, linked with militarism and continuing war, and preparations for conflicts, is a thriving enterprise among the nations. The expansion of unmanned arms delivery systems, such as drones, long-range cruise, and other weapons systems, readily armed with nuclear warheads, is of great concern in times of uncertainty, with political and social unrest. These are the underlying realities of an increasing military expenditure among the world's nations today.

Greet has observed that Christians need to relate their beliefs to the hard actualities of the world.[63] Like Kember, he feels that there is a great need to fire the enthusiasm of younger folk, 'for whom a future free of the horrors of war is hugely important'.[64] He also suggested that with 'the destructive power of modern weaponry it is difficult to see how any modern war could conform to the limiting criteria of "just war" as traditionally defined'.[65]

---

[59] *Fellowship of Reconciliation Peacemaker Briefings* 04, 'Study War No More: Military Involvement in UK Universities' (2007), p. 1, https://www.for.org.uk/wp-content/uploads/2013/11/PB4WEB_0.pdf (accessed 1.6.2012)

[60] *Fellowship of Reconciliation Peacelinks* 30.2 (2016), p. 12.

[61] Stockholm International Peace Research Institute. 'Top Five Countries, Military Expenditure', 2015. global statistics. www.sipri.org/ (Accessed 11.3.2017). Figures are expressed in £'s, using a conversion rate of $1 = £0.82221 (11.3.2017).

[62] Stockholm International Peace Research Institute Statistics. www.sipri.org/ (Accessed 11.3.2017).

[63] Kenneth Greet, 'War and Peace – The Changing Agenda', *P21C*, p. 2, <www.mpf.org.uk> < www.for.org.uk> (Accessed 1.6.2012).

[64] Greet, 'War and Peace – The Changing Agenda', p. 2.

[65] Greet, 'War and Peace – The Changing Agenda', p. 2.

The Roman Catholic educator, Joseph J. Fahey,[66] addressed the confusion that is apparent in many Christian churches, concerning pacifism. He cites the example of a young college student, who asserted:

> I am confused by Christianity today … I don't know whether to be a pacifist, a follower of the just war, a crusader, or a world citizen. All four seem to be Christian positions.[67]

Fahey explained that this confusion is not without basis, as at times the Christian churches have espoused all four viewpoints, with each position having its advocates.[68] Fahey writing almost a century after Booth-Clibborn, identified exactly the same problem: that war and the peaceful alternatives to it are not honestly addressed within the majority of Christian churches.

This chapter has included reflections from several scholars, educators and writers,[69] which span the last century or so of Christian pacifism. Some have attempted to record the treatment of pacifists and conscientious objectors during the two World Wars. They have also placed them within the context of history, militarism, and wider society. A number have stated the case for an unequivocal acceptance of an alternative to war that is based upon their acceptance of Christ's life and teaching.[70] Whilst pacifism has had, arguably, a long and honourable tradition in Britain,[71] the established peace churches, Quaker, Mennonite and Anabaptist, have attempted to maintain their pacifist teaching, and have added to the discussion, the issues of disarmament, justice and poverty. Pacifist groups continue their work within the mainstream Church denominations in the UK, but generally, the Churches have not been, and are not today overtly pacifist. The work of the pacifist institutions

---

[66] Joseph J. Fahey, *Peace, War and the Christian Conscience* (London: Pax Christi, 2003). p. 3

[67] Fahey, *Peace, War and the Christian Conscience*, p. 3.

[68] Fahey, *Peace, War and the Christian Conscience*, p. 3.

[69] Rachel Barker, Brock and Young, Ceadel, Ferguson, and Marwick.

[70] Booth-Clibborn, Richards, Macgregor, Raven, Bainton, Knox, Clark, Desjardins, Clouse, Greet, Mills-Powell, Barrett, Catherwood, Kember, and Fahey.

[71] David Ross, *England, History of a Nation* (New Lanark: Geddes & Grossett, 2008), p. 278.

continues, and has a wide role in voicing issues, such as arms control, nuclear disarmament, and peaceful coexistence.

In 2013, *The Housemans Peace Diary*, celebrated its 60th year of publication, marking its 'attempts to build a better world out of the human and physical wreckage of a major war'.[72] In its significant section entitled, *World Peace Directory*, it 'lists over 1,500 national and international organisations, covering the breadth of the peace movement'.[73]

Global militarisation continues unabated: countries engage repeatedly in war, and continuously make preparations for war; the manufacture of weapons of mass terror and destruction attracts attention in the contemporary news media. At the same time, the voices of dissent against war, bloodshed and violence, around the world, speak out consistently.

---

[72] *Housemans Peace Diary, 2013, with World Peace Directory* (London: House-man, 2013), 'Taking Risks to Resist'.

[73] *Houseman's Peace Diary, 2013, with World Peace Directory*, 'Directory Introduction'.

10

CONCLUSIONS

The early Pentecostal movement in Britain, which soon developed to include four separate strands: Elim, Assemblies of God, the Apostolic Church, and the Church of God, all generally claimed an experience of the Holy Spirit, as outlined in the Book of Acts, together with Spiritual Gifts, and Fruit, as taught by the Apostle Paul in his Letters. Pacifism, rather than patriotism/militarism, was integral to the beliefs and practice of the Early Church. Early Church pacifism survived, intact, until the time of Constantine (307-337). Pacifism then enjoyed something of a renaissance with the Mennonites, and later with George Fox, and the early Quakers (the Society of Friends) in seventeenth-century England. Clive Barrett has identified pacifism, from the times of the Early Church, and has traced this, as a virtually unbroken strand through Christian history.[1] Radical Christianity, as claimed by George Fox and the early Quakers, and later by A.S. Booth-Clibborn, included pacifism as a legacy from the times of the first Christians. The essential nature of the Pentecostal movement in its early years was radical, Christ-centred, and Bible-focussed, in its leadership, fellowship, worship, and ministries.

Quakers at the time of Fox sought only to have the mind of Christ; this was for them incompatible with war and bloodshed. Fox's enduring legacy is in the way that he provided a relevant model of prophetic, Spirit-empowered and enabled ministry for the

---

[1] Peace Tax Seven Website: www.peacetaxseven.com/anglican.html (accessed 18.4.2017).

contemporary Church of Jesus Christ worldwide. It was no accident that A.S. Booth-Clibborn viewed the pacifist faith of his early Quakerism as a non-negotiable of the Christian gospel and encouraged pacifism when he joined in fellowship with the early Pentecostal movement in Britain. His legacy suggests that he was a serious influence upon many young people within Pentecostalism. Booth-Clibborn based his Christian pacifist faith upon both the Old and New Testaments, upon the overt teaching of Jesus, upon the evidence of the Early Church's practice up to the time of Constantine, upon the evidence of the Church Fathers, upon his Quaker ancestry, and upon the views of a number of key historical figures. Booth-Clibborn was described by his wife Kate as an ardent (passionate, zealous) pacifist.

Alexander Boddy defended the 'just war' position, and as a patriot he saw no problem with supporting war. In his role as a voluntary chaplain in WWI, he encouraged the troops. This was at serious odds with Booth-Clibborn's view that to encourage men to believe in the shed blood of Jesus Christ for salvation one day, and then to cheer them on in a savage charge to shed the blood of fellow-men and fellow-Christians the next day; he could not find adequate words to fit the case. Booth-Clibborn, remarking on the work of the chaplaincy, suggested that inasmuch as they were unable to save men *from* war, they sought to save them *in* war. Fielden has suggested that many Anglican clergymen were convinced of the righteousness of the British cause in the Great War, Boddy also. At this time, pacifism was not viewed favourably by the majority of ministers within the Anglican Church in Britain. Boddy went along with many of his Anglican peers and showed little patience with those of pacifist faith and persuasion within early Pentecostalism. Frequently in *Confidence*, Boddy's Pentecostal newspaper, he disregarded the pacifist point of view, and on the few occasions that he allowed a reference to it, he immediately sought to invalidate the position, by publishing contrary views, in the same issue. In short, he failed to engage with, or accommodate those of the Christian pacifist persuasion within Pentecostalism.

Christian leaders and believers are ultimately accountable as to how they appropriate the teaching of Jesus Christ. Jesus left a serious reminder that his Word 'will never pass away' (Mt. 24.35). John announced that Jesus brings a new age of 'grace and truth' (Jn 1.14). For the Christian, Jesus has come in order to supersede, surpass, and fulfil the Law. It is from him that the Church takes it mandate; it either builds upon the rock-like certainty of his teaching, or the sand-like insecurity and uncertainty of its rejection.

Booth-Clibborn consecrated his life to what he called the war of redemption. His Christian pacifism was contrary in nature to wars of aggression. He asserted that Pentecostal baptisms of fire are the exact opposite of the fiery baptisms of war, and that lies, untruths and fabrication are all obligatory in war, and that it is anti-Christian.

The life and ministry of George Fox brings together several themes that were integral within early Pentecostalism in Britain: Christ-centred and Word-centred preaching, prophecy, healing, and not least pacifism that was borne of Fox's understanding of the mind of Jesus Christ. One could add, as far as Fox's experience was concerned, the work of the Holy Spirit helped him to open up the Word in order to communicate it effectively to his listeners, and to 'read' hostile crowds that wished him harm. This would now refer to as discernment or a word of knowledge.

Barrett has verified that at the time of WWI, within Anglicanism, there were those who were of pacifist persuasion. This is corroborated by Ceadel in his statistics.[2] Much later, in 1937, the Anglican Pacifist Fellowship (APF) was formed, and today has of the order of 1100 members across 40 countries. The APF's aims are to reject war as a means of solving international disputes, and to believe that peace and justice should be sought by non-violent means.[3] The APF's key beliefs are that Jesus' teaching is incompatible with the waging of war, that a Christian Church should never support or justify war, and that our Christian witness should include opposing the waging or justifying of war.[4]

In the USA, Paul N. Alexander in his substantial, scholarly work, *Peace to War*,[5] traces within the Pentecostal group, the Assemblies of God, through the twentieth century up to more recent times, the

---

[2] See Chapter 9.

[3] Anglican Pacifist Fellowship Website: www.anglicanpeacemaker.org.uk (accessed 18.4.2017).

[4] Anglican Pacifist Fellowship Website (accessed 18.4.2017).

[5] Paul N. Alexander, *Peace to War: Shifting Allegiances in the Assemblies of God* (Scottdale, PA: Herald Press, 2009), p. 350.

gradual shift away from its early heritage of pacifist faith. Alexander also reports on the work of Pentecostals and Charismatics for Peace and Justice, an organisation currently devoted to 'work and pray together for peace and justice',[6] in which he seeks to be a just peacemaker.

He writes:

> The second century of Pentecostalism is just beginning, and perhaps it can bear witness to the re-emergence of a powerful Pentecostal peace-with-justice witness that blesses the world far beyond what we could ever imagine.[7]

Numerous wars continue around the world, and many nations are engaged with building up their military capabilities, continuously preparing for war. Today, in Britain, pacifism is recognised as a mainstream Anglican position, though not yet a dominant belief of the faith.[8] Ironically, within Pentecostalism in Britain today, although its entire pacifist history has yet to be written (from WWI, up to the present time), it is not appropriate to draw premature conclusions. The reality, however, is that one might today struggle to find pacifist faith, or an anti-war stance among its churches in Britain. In recent times, some of the Pentecostal movement's publications have included articles on military chaplaincy, military leadership, and pro-war articles.

Patriotism and militarism are widely accepted in our day and time, in both church and society. It is not unheard of that national and political leaders might even contemplate leading their country to war, on the basis that their own personal popularity or the fortunes of their particular political party, is waning. There is an expectation that militarism and war unify a nation. In many national and international disputes, war is often viewed as a first means of settling differences and disputes, rather than a last recourse.

At times the problem of war in the Old Testament is not addressed in any meaningful way, and is often referred to in isolation from New Testament teachings. On this Philip Jensen has introduced an appropriate insight. He writes:

---

[6] Alexander, *Peace to War*, p. 349.

[7] Alexander, *Peace to War*, p. 350.

[8] Peace Tax Seven Website: www.peacetaxseven.com/anglican.html (accessed 18.4.2017).

The coming of Christ has transformed key elements of the identity of the people of God. They are no longer defined by race or by land, but by faith in Jesus Christ. The radical change in dispensation following Easter means that there is no warrant for applying nationalistic aspects of the Old Testament, including the Yahweh war, to the church.[9]

This outlines an appropriate hermeneutic, applicable to this theme, for Christians today.

Although Days of Remembrance are commemorated annually in Britain, and whilst they are treated solemnly and with respect, they sadly fail to produce a will, among many political and national leaders, to work to eliminate war and militarism around the world. It is today widely feared that the world is an increasingly unsafe place.

Whilst it is predominantly the responsibility of ordained ministers, pastors, and teachers, to teach the Good News of Jesus Christ systematically in our Churches, it is not really appropriate to avoid Jesus' pacifist teaching, simply because it is contrary to what has become accepted as expedient around the world.[10] Generally the message of Jesus as the Prince of Peace (Isa. 9.6), and as the one did no violence, and whose mouth knew no deceit (Isa. 53.9), has been lost, with few exceptions to the Church. This message surfaces, mainly in the Christmas period, if at all. Churches do, however, make much of their annual November Remembrance Day services, but these are not usually for the purpose of introducing themes of the new order of God's kingdom of peace, non-violence, and justice, as inaugurated by Jesus.

The task of changing the direction of the Churches, to include pro-active, pacifist and non-violent faith is a major undertaking, but not impossible. This has little to do with left-wing politics, but rather being faithful to the teaching of Jesus. Fahey has suggested that a whole process of re-education is needed. Among the principles that he has suggested (and these are applicable to Church and wider society) are that we promote peace through education, that we break the link that exists between violence and courage, that we

---

[9] Philip Jenson, The *Problem of War in the Old Testament* (Cambridge: Grove Books, 2010), p. 26.

[10] See Chapter 7, for discussion.

convince others that war is not noble or glorious, that we shape public opinion, and that we examine our faith.[11]

We must reflect on the fact that few Christian Churches are active in the areas of pacifism, peace, and non-violence. The Pentecostal and Charismatic Churches in Britain, who are part of the world's fastest-growing faith group, appears to have little or no voice in the vital area of national and global peace-making.

This book has been written in order to present a challenge to Christians, especially those who claim to be Pentecostal and Charismatic, and who believe that they are in continuity with the Early Church, to reflect upon their legacy, in attempting to communicate a consistent, relevant, radical, and contemporary message today.

---

[11] Fahey, *Peace, War, and the Christian Conscience*, pp. 22-23.

BIBLIOGRAPHY

Books:

Alexander, Paul N., *Peace to War: Shifting Allegiances in the Assemblies of God* (Scottdale, PA: Herald Press, 2009).

Anderson, Allan, *Spreading Fires – The Missionary Nature of Early Pentecostalism* (London: SCM, 2007).

Bainton, Roland H., *Christian Attitudes to War and Peace* (London: Hodder & Stoughton, 1961).

Barker, Rachel, *Conscience, Government and War, Conscientious Objection in Great Britain 1939-1945* (London: Routledge & Kegan Paul, 1982).

Barclay, Robert, *The Inner Life of the Religious Societies of the Commonwealth* (London: H&S, c1876).

Booth, Catherine, *A Poet of Praise: A Tribute to Arthur Sydney Booth-Clibborn* (London: Marshall, Morgan & Scott, c.1939).

Booth-Clibborn, A.S., *Blood Against Blood* (New York: Charles Cook, 1914).

Brock, Peter, & Nigel Young, *Pacifism in the Twentieth Century* (New York: Syracuse University Press, 1999).

Cadbury, H.J., *George Fox's 'Book of Miracles'* (Philadelphia: QUIP, 2000).

Carson, D.A., *et al.* (eds.), *New Bible Commentary* (IVP: Leicester, 1994).

Ceadel, Martin, *Pacifism in Britain 1914–1945: The Defining of a Faith* (Oxford: Clarendon Press, 1980).

Catherwood, Christopher, *Why the Nations Rage* (London: Hodder & Stoughton, 1997).

Clark, Robert, *Does the Bible Teach Pacifism?* (London: Marshall's Paperbacks, 1976, 1983).

Barrett, Clive (ed.), *Peace Together, A Vision of Christian Pacifism* (Cambridge: James Clarke & Co., 1987).

Clouse, Robert G. (ed.), *War, Four Christian Views* (Downers Grove, IL: IVP, 1981).

Crockfords Clerical Directory (London: Horace Cox, 1880).

Desjardins, Michel, *Peace, Violence and the New Testament* (Sheffield: Sheffield Academic Press, 1997).

Durnbaugh, Donald, *The Believers' Church* (Scottdale, PA: Herald Press, 1968, 1985).

Edwards, D.L., *Christianity The First Two Thousand Years* (London: Cassell, 1997).

Fahey, Joseph, J., *Peace, War, and the Christian Conscience* (London: Pax Christi UK, 2003).

Ferguson, Niall, *The Pity of War* (London: Penguin, 1998).

Fox, George, *George Fox's Journal* (London: Isbister, 1905).

Gardner, J., & N. Wenborn (eds.), *History Today Companion to British History* (London: Collins & Brown, 1995).

Gee, Donald, *Wind and Flame* (Croydon: Heath Press, 1967).

Goddard, Andrew, *When is War Justified?* (Cambridge: Grove Books, 2003).

Greet, Kenneth, *The Big Sin* (London: Marshall Morgan & Scott, 1982).

Hey, David, *How our Ancestors Lived: A History of Life a Hundred Years Ago* (Kew: The National Archives, 2003).

Holy Bible; New International Version (London: International Bible Society / Hodder & Stoughton, 1999).

Hilton, James, *Goodbye, Mr Chipps* (London: Hodder & Stoughton, 1934).

Hirst, M.E., *The Quakers in Peace and War* (London: Swarthmore Press, 1923).

Jenson, Philip, *The Problem of War in the Old Testament* (Cambridge: Grove Books, 2002, 2010).

Kay, William K., and Anne E. Dyer, *Pentecostal and Charismatic Studies* (London: SCM Press, 2004).

Klassen, Walter, *Anabaptism in Outline* (Ontario: Herald Press, 1981).

Knox, John D., *Eternal War, the Why of Conscientious Objection* (Victoria, Australia: New Life Publications, 1967).

Macgregor, G.H.C., *The New Testament Basis of Christian Pacifism* (London: Fellowship of Reconciliation, 1936, 1953).

Malcomson, Keith, *Pentecostal Pioneers Remembered* (Longwood, USA: Xulon Press, 2008).

Marwick, Arthur, *A History of the Modern British Isles, 1914–1999: Circumstances, Events and Outcomes* (Oxford: Blacknell, 2000).

Milne, Bruce, *Know the Truth* (Leicester: IVP, 1982).

Moo, J. Donald, 'Romans' in Carson, D.A., France, R.T., Motyer, J.A., & Wenham, G.J. (eds.), *New Bible Commentary 21st Century Edition* (Leicester: IVP, 1994).

Mills-Powell, Dana (ed.), *Decide for Peace* (Basingstoke: Marshall Morgan & Scott, 1986).

New English Dictionary and Thesaurus (New Lanark, Scotland: Geddes and Grosset Ltd, 1995).

Noble, V., *The Man in Leather Breeches* (London: Elek, 1953).

Perry, Melanie (ed.), 'Anne Askew', *Chambers Biographical Dictionary* (London: Chambers & Harrap, 1997), p. 191.

Raven, Charles, *The Theological Basis of Christian Pacifism* (London: The Fellowship of Reconciliation, 1952).

Richards, Leyton, *The Christian's Alternative to War* (London: Student Christian Movement Press, 1929, 1935).

Ross, David, *England, History of a Nation* (New Lanark: Geddes & Grossett, 2008).

Scott, Carolyn, *The Heavenly Witch: The Story of the Maréchale* (London: Hamish Hamilton, 1981).

Sharman, C.W., *George Fox and the Quakers* (London: QHS, 1991).

Stott, John, *Issues Facing Christians Today* (London: Marshall Pickering, 1990).

Todman, Dan, *The Great War – Myth and Memory* (London: Hambledon Continuum, 2005).

Unknown author, *I Am Persuaded* (New Malden: Fellowship of Reconciliation, 1956, 1958, 1970).

Wakefield, Gavin, *Alexander Boddy Pentecostal Anglican Pioneer* (London: Paternoster, 2007).

—*The First Pentecostal Anglican* (Cambridge: Grove Books, 2001).

Other Sources:

Alexander, Paul N., 'Historical and Theological Origins of Assemblies of God' in *Quaker Theology* 12.1 (2005-2006), p. 3. quest@quaker. org (accessed 1/6/2013).

Anglican Pacifist Website: www.anglicanpeacemaker.org.uk (accessed 18.4.2017).

Boddy, A.A., (editor & publisher), *Confidence*, All Issues, (1908–1926).

Boddy, Jane Vazeille, 'Alexander Alfred Boddy', Biographical Notes.

Bock, Cherice, 'Quakers on the Spectrum of Nonviolence: In Conversation with K. Barth, Reinhold Niebuhr, J.H. Yoder, M.L. King Jr., and Robert Barclay', *Quaker Religious Thought* 110.2 (2008). http://digitalcommons.georgefox.edu/qrt/vol110/iss1/2 (Accessed 1.9.2016).

Booth-Clibborn, A. S., *Blood Against Blood*, digital version accessible at Cornell University Library, http://archive.org./details/cu31924029 1613.

Craven, G., 'George Fox, Quaker leader, Man of the Spirit', *Journal of the European Pentecostal Theological Association* 29.1 (2009), pp. 56-71.

—'Drawn to the Father's Son', *Heroes of the Faith* 12 (Oct–Dec. 2012), pp. 14-17.

Fielden, Kevin Christopher, 'The Church of England in the First World War', Electronic Theses and Dissertations, Paper 1080 (2005). http://dc.etsu/etd/1080 (Accessed 1.1.2015).

Flower Pentecostal Heritage Centre, USA. www.ifphc.org (Accessed 1.1. 2016).

Fellowship of Reconciliation, Peacemaker Briefings 04. (2007), p. 1. www.for. org.uk (accessed 1.6.2014).

Fellowship of Reconciliation, Peacelinks 30.2 (Summer 2016), p. 1 www.for.org. uk (accessed 1.6.2014).

Greet, Kenneth, *P21C* (32 (July 2009), p. 1, <www.mpf.org.uk> (accessed 1.6.2012).

Greet, Kenneth, 'War and Peace – The Changing Agenda', *P21C*, p. 2, www.mpf.org.uk ; www.for.org.uk (Accessed 1.6.2014).

Guiton, G., 'Seventeenth Century Quaker Pacifism', *Reviews in Religion and Theology*, 9.4 (Sept. 2002), pp. 290-96.

Housemans Peace Diary, 2013, with World Peace Directory (London: Houseman, 2013).

Kember, Norman, *Baptist Peace Fellowship Newsletter* (Spring 2014), p. 2. www.bpf.org.uk (accessed 1.6.2012).

Massey, Richard D., 'Sound and Scriptural Union' (PhD Thesis, Birmingham University, 1987).

Peace Tax Seven Website: www.peacetaxseven.com/anglican.html (accessed 18.4.2017).

Redemption Tidings, Assemblies of God Publication, All Issues, 1924–1985.

Robinson, James, 'Arthur Booth-Clibborn: Pentecostal Patriarch', *Journal of the European Pentecostal Theological Association* 21 (2001), pp. 68-90.

Stockholm International Peace Research Institute. 'Top Five Countries, Military Expenditure', 2015. Global Statistics. www.sipri.org/ (Accessed 11.3.2017).

van der Laan, Cornelis, 'Alexander Boddy: Anglican Father of Dutch Pentecostalism', *Journal of the European Pentecostal Theological Association* 31.1 (2011), pp. 93-110.

INDEX OF BIBLICAL REFERENCES

INDEX OF AUTHORS